Ethics and Excuses

ETHICS AND EXCUSES

The Crisis in Professional Responsibility

Banks McDowell

Quorum Books
Westport, Connecticut • London

Library of Congress Cataloging-in-Publication Data

McDowell, Banks.
    Ethics and excuses : the crisis in professional responsibility / Banks McDowell.
      p. cm.
    Includes bibliographical references and index.
    ISBN 1–56720–386–8 (alk. paper)
    1. Ethics—United States. 2. Responsibility—United States. 3. Excuses. I. Title.
BJ352.M39 2000
174—dc21   99–462239

British Library Cataloguing in Publication Data is available.

Library of Congress Catalog Card Number: 99–462239
ISBN 1–56720–386–8

First published in 2000

Quorum Books, 88 Post Road West, Westport, CT 06881
An imprint of Greenwood Publishing Group, Inc.
www.quorumbooks.com

Printed in the United States of America

The paper used in this book complies with the
Permanent Paper Standard issued by the National
Information Standards Organization (Z39.48–1984).

10 9 8 7 6 5 4 3 2 1

Contents

Preface

The genesis of this book belongs in large measure to discussions with students. In the course of teaching for nearly forty years in five different law schools, I noticed three traits widely held by students.

First, many had difficulty thinking in terms of probabilities. Everything had to be true or false, right or wrong, black or white. Subtleties, uncertainties, and complexities disturbed them mightily. If professional ethics pose difficult, nonstandard, and complex problems, which cannot be dealt with by clear rules or bright line analysis, these students are ill equipped to deal with them.

Second, most students were indifferent about ethical issues, except at the most general level. Their attitude is best described as "amoral," rather than "immoral." Ethical problems are seldom discussed in public arenas or private conversations. Some students were deeply concerned with morality, but their attitudes tended to be held privately and muted in the public forum of professional school.

Finally, there was an almost universal propensity to offer excuses, however implausible, whenever they did not perform properly, whether it was handing in a late paper, being unprepared for class, giving a less than satisfactory answer, or failing an examination. There was a reluctance to take personal responsibility for their failings, or offer apologies.

And yet nearly all these students were above average in intelligence, well educated according to current standards, and appeared to be decent. The contradictions between their behavior in avoiding responsibility and my perception of them as basically decent always puzzled me. The practice of giving and accepting excuses is the most fruitful point to explore these inconsistencies. While excuses are ubiquitous in our dealings with each other, they are seldom formally discussed in the field of ethics or informally when people converse with each other. An excuse is given. It is summarily accepted or rejected, and there the matter ends.

A more basic paradox underlying the practice of giving and accepting excuses is that all human beings have competing impulses, which are rarely resolved satisfactorily. One is a genuine desire to be decent, ethical, trustworthy, and generous, living up to the aspirations that represent the good. However, each of us is capable of acting in ways that are egotistical, mean, and destructive to ourselves and others, traits we label as bad. Each one in the project of constructing his own life, and each society in struggling toward maintaining viable ways of functioning, face this eternal human conflict. A major indicator of where the struggle occurs and how it is progressing is the type and amount of excuses we offer ourselves and others.

This book is about practical ethics and more specifically professional ethics, a subcategory of practical ethics. For whom is the book written? Stated differently, what sort of reader do I have in mind? As an academic, it would be natural to address specialists in professional ethics, those who teach and write about the theoretical problems. My main concern, however, is to describe real problems professionals face and discuss how such problems are or might be dealt with by individual professionals and by society. In a rapidly changing and ever more complex world, the discussion has to be rooted in the reality of the world where students and practitioners must function.

One aspect of this analysis will be a comparison between legal defenses and ethical excuses. Lawyers have something to learn from ethical theory, and ethicists much to learn from legal experiences. In addition, ordinary people who themselves not only use excuses freely, but are also on the receiving end of professionals' excuses, have something to learn from lawyers and ethical theorists.

I owe greater debts than I can acknowledge to many people who supported me, stimulated my thoughts, or contributed ideas, which I could then develop. Some of the more important were Robert Baum, whose comments on my preliminary paper, "The Excuses that Make Professional Ethics Irrelevant," not only made that a better piece, but stimulated further thoughts developed here. Another is George Hole, who responded to that paper in ways that helped me see ramifications of some problems of excuses. A valuable insight came from a former secretary, Leslie Vigus, who showed me how closely excuses used by professionals track with those used by her teen-age daughters. Hans Mohr made clear the important difference between apology and excuse, and the value that apology has in many cultures for dealing with problems we associate with excuses. He also helped me see more explicitly the tensions, if not total inconsistencies, between ethical behavior and economically efficient commercial activity. Sheila Reynolds, a former colleague, who teaches professional responsibility at Washburn Law School, gave me examples of excuses as well as citations to authorities. Mark Weisberg, in a critical reading of part of an earlier draft, helped tighten my language and analysis.

A great debt is owed to J. L. Austin, whose brilliant and provocative paper "A Plea for Excuses" was brought to my attention by Joel Levin after I had begun this project. I am not sure I say much that was not already anticipated in an abbreviated fashion in that spectacular essay.

A great and immeasurable debt is owed my wife, Ellen, who helped me to understand a culture other than my own and see a side of life more intuitive and aesthetic than my own personality and upbringing would allow. Furthermore, she has spent more than forty years listening to my excuses and reacting to them, sometimes with sympathy and often enough critically, so that I have had to take her opinions seriously.

As a teacher, I developed a style of analysis and discussion that strove for dialogue with my students. It emphasized my personal reaction to problems and tried to show the complexities of individual contexts of choice, rather than trying to always be objective, impersonal, and offering simple solutions. In trying to understand this world and its challenges, asking the right questions always seemed more important than finding the "right" answers. This was an invitation to my students to do the same. My preference for this approach to analyzing and communicating will be found throughout the following pages. It may make this book appear too personal and anecdotal, but whether or not there are true observations and analysis here depends on whether it is supported by the reader's experiences and observations, rather than by social science findings. Social science research is needed in the area of excuses, but I am not the person with the interest or the skills to undertake that project.

Finally, a comment on linguistic style. A book on ethics focuses inevitably on an individual accused of acting (or failing to act) in a way labeled unethical. I refer to that person either as the "actor" or, since this is about professional ethics, as the "professional." This individual focus may give rise to gender bias. While the actor can be either male or female, my generation was conditioned to use the male pronoun as the generic singular designation. I have tried in the past to overcome that by using plurals, difficult in this context, or using the female pronoun exclusively, which is an overcorrection. Here I use the singular male or female pronouns randomly and, I hope, equally.

1

Introduction: The Ethical Crisis?

There seems to be a growing consensus that our society faces a crisis in professional ethics. While this may be a subset of a more general crisis in ethical responsibility, my primary interest is in professionals, who are traditionally expected, or at least claim, to display a higher level of ethics than the general population. Much of my analysis in this book may apply, however, not only to professionals and the excuses given when it is claimed they have acted unethically, but to everyone.

There is certainly unease about professional ethics, not only by the professionals themselves, but by the general public, who are the clients or consumers of professional services. In recent decades, more courses about ethics have been introduced into professional schools. Professional associations are worried about the public image of professionals as being unethical. Books about professional ethics are proliferating.

There are serious issues captured in the statement "There is an ethical crisis for professionals." There is, however, confusion about exactly what those problems may be. Five years ago, I prepared a presentation for an ethics conference entitled "The Excuses that Make Professional Ethics Irrelevant." My thesis was that for ethics, the norms are largely matters of voluntary compliance and if an actor can find excuses that justify to himself those of his actions that might be labeled unethical, the ethical requirements lose force. The more I worked with that notion, the more I discovered that excuses serve not only the function of avoiding ethical responsibility, which is the way we usually think about them, but they are also useful in deciding how to apply and adapt ethical norms in specific contexts. In addition, they point to problems of dysfunction between ethical standards and the needs and problems of contemporary professional practice.

In this chapter, I want to introduce three preliminary questions, which will affect the discussion throughout the book. When we consider whether there is a crisis in professional responsibility, there are ambiguities built into all the central terms. First, when we talk about professionals, whom do we mean? Second, are there special ethical obligations for professionals as distinguished from their legal duties or from their ethical duties as ordinary people? Third, is there really an ethical crisis and if so, how ought we to try to resolve it? The chapter closes with a discussion of why excuses may be a good focal point for considering what the ethical problems and solutions might be. The search for answers to these questions is the purpose of the entire study, so here I merely outline the difficulties inherent in the basic assumption that we are facing an ethical crisis.

WHO COUNT AS PROFESSIONALS?

Out of the workforce, who should be regarded as professionals? It is possible to limit this category of professional to the old traditional groups of high-prestige workers, primarily medical doctors, theologians, university professors, and lawyers. The last fifty years have seen an enormous increase in the professionalization of work. Most skilled service personnel today consider themselves professionals, or aspire to be so considered. Beyond the traditional professions, the list of claimants, hardly complete, would include accountants, journalists, engineers, architects, nurses, schoolteachers, librarians, business managers, financial consultants, and social workers.

Among the insignia of professionalism are formal training, usually in a university, a professional organization, technical journals, and adoption of a code of ethics.[1] For most significant occupations in the modern workforce, there are specialized skills, a need to exercise independent and sound judgment, and some formalization of the process of mastering and improving these skills. If participation in the modern workforce requires specialized training and possession of expertise shared only by each particular group of workers, and for which they are consulted by others, what then distinguishes "professional" from nonprofessional expertise? It could be the relationship between the expert and the one who consults her, a relationship requiring trust because the "client" has to rely on the information given by the expert. Ethical requirements applying to professionals are all based on this inequality of knowledge and the necessity to trust the expert. Accepting these ethical responsibilities could be that characteristic that shifts the worker from being just an employee or a mere accumulator of wealth into the category of true professional. Of course, some traditional professionals display little of this expected ethical character, while workers not normally considered professional may display high qualities of fidelity to customers, a concern about public service over private gain, and a desire to do high-quality work.

Unfortunately, we increasingly define professionals solely in terms of the particular expertise they possess. A lawyer knows the law and how to protect people's rights. A doctor knows her medical specialty and how to cure sick people. An accountant knows how to keep accurate records and tell clients and others what sort of financial shape the client is in. An engineer knows how to work out problems of design and production.

Earlier, we would talk about the character of a lawyer, a doctor, or a minister. By character, we meant the values and traditions shared by members of that particular profession, which defined the kind of choices they made and the sort of person they were in their role as that particular kind of professional. The ethics of the profession and of individual practitioners were an important part of this character. In earlier times, there was quite explicit modeling, if not training, in professional character as well as professional expertise. Over the past half century, formal professional education in the universities has left the character issue largely in the background, so young aspirants have had to pick up the traits of being an ethical professional without much explicit guidance.

In addition to the requirement of exceptional ethics and specialized expertise, one might add the quality of social respect or prestige. One reason that the more traditional professionals want to limit the class and its concomitant privileges is that the broader the category, the less special any particular group of workers will appear to be and the less persuasive the claim of a superior class of worker will be.

Because it is central to my later analysis, I want to mention that one other important attribute professionals claim is autonomy, that is, freedom from outside regulation. It is argued that professionals possess a special expertise and that the use of that expertise on behalf of clients should largely be left free of controls, whether from governmental or legal regulation, from the supervision of employers, from the unsophisticated demands of clients, or from monitoring by third-party payers, such as insurers. Some of the excuses used by contemporary professionals raise serious questions about the degree to which that claimed autonomy might be largely illusory.

"Professional" is a term of approbation and of respect. What classes of workers and what individuals within those groups are entitled to that description is an important question, as a matter both of theory and of practical consequences. It is central to the problems of this book, but cannot at this early stage be adequately resolved.

WHAT ARE PROFESSIONAL ETHICS?

When we discuss professional ethics, we need to know not only whom we mean by "professional," but also what we mean by "ethics?" Does being ethical for a professional represent something significantly different from being a normal economic actor, or from the ethics we expect of nonprofessionals? As we increasingly move to a service economy, what most people do to earn their living is relational and involves dealing with other people. However, the notion that the fundamental economic activity is making things, manufacturing or farming, has not lost its analytical grip on us. This can distort how we think about economic activity. One does not normally talk about the relational or ethical obligations of farmers, miners, assembly line workers, or cabinetmakers. However, when we describe someone selling a service, we must discuss relational (and ethical) issues.

Are the ethical requirements for computer programmers who help customers work out their record-keeping problems fundamentally different from those for accountants, or is the work of auto mechanics who help people keep their automobiles running fundamentally different from that of engineers helping entrepreneurs work out how to produce a product more efficiently? Since my concern is excuses, particularly those used when actors are accused of acting unethically, are there differences between the ethical responsibilities of auto mechanics or computer programmers and those of newer professions like accounting and engineering or the more traditional professions of medicine and law?

The issue of whether professional ethics means unique ethical requirements applying only to those professional roles or refers to all the ethical obligations from whatever source impinging on those people designated as professionals will be a continuing question throughout the book. My preference is to use the broader definition of professional ethics because some of the very serious professional conflicts producing excuses can be understood only when we see there are clashes among ethical systems.

In order to give a context for discussing ethical excuses, it helps to have a general notion of basic professional ethical duties. Some of the major ones are (a) to protect the interests and welfare of the client, (b) to be loyal and not to engage in conflicts of interests by preferring the interests of other clients or those of the professional himself over that owed the particular client, (c) to protect confidential information the client gives to the professional, (d) not to appropriate or misuse the client's property, and (e) to perform the professional services requested by the client competently or else find another professional specialist who can do so.

Ethical issues giving rise to excuses are almost always relational problems, and those of us who cannot lay claim to being professionals usually have relationships with a number of people holding themselves out as such. Are ethical responsibilities substantially different depending on which end of the relationship you find yourself? Does the client owe the professional a lesser degree of loyalty or honesty or confidentiality? Whether professional or not, we are all involved in professional ethics. And certainly the role of excuses is no different whether they come from the side of the professional or that of the client. Even if the ethical duties of the client are not the same as those of the professional, I will argue in the final chapter that as the victims of unethical activity, clients or others coming in contact with the professional owe an ethical responsibility in the way the excuse is responded to.

Another important issue to be aware of in the definition of "ethics" in professional activity is the zone of operations for professional ethics. There seems to be a confusion between the law of professional practice, which is the subject of much of what is taught in courses on "professional ethics," and ethical performance within the zone of professional autonomy, which I will argue is the primary area of ethical concern. These matters are the subject matter of Chapter 4.

WHAT IS THE NATURE OF THE ETHICAL CRISIS?

One important question that is difficult to deal with is whether there is in fact an ethical crisis. A crisis is "an unstable or crucial time or state of affairs in which a decisive change is pending: esp: one with the distinct possibility of a highly undesirable outcome."[2] If the incidence of unethical activity among professionals is no worse than it has been over a long period of time, one could not properly speak of a crisis. Of course, the degree of unethical activity may have been unsatisfactory or deplorable over the entire period.[3] Are the ethical practices of professionals today substantially worse than they would have been four decades or a century ago? This is difficult to answer because unethical conduct is often hidden, expectations may have altered over that period, and the role of the media in informing the public about unethical actions of prominent people has become more pervasive. Any of these factors make gathering reliable information difficult. Just as political figures must now lead an almost blameless life to avoid being stigmatized as dishonest or unethical, so must well-known professionals.

Whether it is factually so or not, there is a feeling today that the ethical practices of professionals, and of everybody else, have gotten worse. That perception is to a great extent the reality that professionals must deal with.

The common strategy for coping with the perception that an ethical crisis exists is to increase ethics instruction in the professional schools and to require continuing education programs devoted to ethics. For lawyers, the profession I know best, this process began with Watergate because of the large number of lawyers involved in that cover-up. With each new revelation of a well-known lawyer charged with unethical activity, the demand increases for more ethics instruction, although one can be skeptical about the degree to which the law schools have fulfilled that demand.

The governing assumption seems to be that those professionals acting unethically must not know what their ethical duties are and need to be taught them. A more sophisticated, and cynical, variant of this approach is that professionals need to be warned about transgressions that will be taken seriously and could lead to severe sanctions.

The widely held public perception that professionals are unethical is not based on a belief that professionals, or their clients, are unclear about what ethical conduct is, but rather that professionals do not act ethically. It appears to be more a problem of compliance than of incomplete knowledge.[4] When I began this project, I shared that belief. I now think the ethical difficulties professionals face are more complex than just a mere failure to comply with clear ethical injunctions.

At the outset, one should take a tentative position on whether the problem underlying the "crisis" is that ethical standards (1) are unknown and unclear, (2) are clear and usually followed, (3) are clear, but widely disregarded, or (4) contain elements of all three possibilities. Which hypothesis we select will not only control how we analyze the crisis in professional ethics, but how we organize analysis or empirical research and what types of solutions we seek.

If the problem were lack of clarity in standards, better ethical formulation and education would be the answer. This seems to be the assumption of many professional educators, which is not surprising given their role as teachers.

If the standards are clear and generally followed, but disregarded by the bad apples in the professional barrel, the solution would be a public relations campaign to acquaint the public with the true extent of ethical conduct coupled with vigorous enforcement of the standards against those professionals who disregard them.

If the standards are clear but widely disregarded, this would seem to indicate either that the standards are inappropriate or that our professions are filled with immoral or amoral people. It would then be necessary to concentrate on redesigning institutional structures and working relationships so that untrustworthy professionals have little opportunity to do damage, a formidable design problem. Such a solution would have to constrain professional autonomy and minimize the opportunity for innovation, as well as provide stringent and obtrusive monitoring.

A possible explanation for much unethical activity by professionals is that it is caused by dysfunctional social structures or by questionable contemporary cultural values, which seem to make the standards irrelevant or difficult to comply with, rather than by individual immorality. If so, expectations ought to be reformulated and the way professional services are delivered substantially altered.

My starting assumption was the qualified third position; that is, the standards are generally understood and widely ignored, but this failure to comply is mainly the result of structural problems in the way that professionals are organized and services are delivered, as well as due to changes in the values of the larger society in which professionals function. That perception underlay an earlier book in which I explored the problem of the delivery of excessive or unnecessary services by many professionals.[5] I concluded that this activity was produced in large part by pressures to compete and be financially successful.

There are two arguments for the assumption that the ethical problems of professionals in the contemporary world are not primarily due to lack of knowledge. The first is that in the informal dialogue between victims of unethical activity and the professional actors, the accused professional seldom takes the strong position that there is no such thing as professional ethical obligations, or the weaker position (described in Chapter 3 as one of the excuses) that he did not know of the specific obligation. Instead, he gives an avoidance or mitigating excuse.

The other is a more subtle argument based on the levels of guilt carried by many individual professionals for the moral quality of how they practice their profession. If they did not suspect their actions were often immoral or might be so, they would not feel guilt. They would also not need to give excuses. There is no requirement to feel remorse or excuse yourself for not complying with obligations you are not aware you have.

My set of starting assumptions in this book may well be influenced by the fact I was trained as a lawyer and taught law students for thirty-seven years. Compliance problems are a lawyer's concern, but not the major concern of academic theorists.[6] Whenever the public feels actors are failing in their social and ethical responsibilities, there is a demand for the legal system to codify the duties and then use legal enforcement to compel obedience. This has happened in professional ethics not only with the formulation of codes of ethics, but also by means of specialized statutes defining ethical standards for professionals.[7] Professional ethics might well be analyzed as a subfield of law where the norms function as legal rules, rather than as ethical principles. One distinguishing characteristic of law is that norm violation carries state-imposed sanctions. Suspension of licenses or probationary procedures by governmental agencies are examples of such sanctions. Malpractice actions in civil courts may also be designed to compel compliance with certain ethical concepts, particularly the one that requires professionals to meet acceptable levels of professional competence. The issue of whether professional ethics ought to be thought of as a legal, rather than an ethical system, will be discussed in more detail in Chapter 4.

THE CENTRAL IMPORTANCE OF EXCUSES

If one accepts tentatively my assumption that the real ethical problems facing professionals are not ones of learning what ethical standards are, but of living up to them, then there should be more focus on the excuses offered and accepted for lapses from ethical standards.

While excuses are always important, they are more significant in this time of apparent crisis. The first reason is a formal one. Any ethical system that does not account for acceptable excuses is incomplete. In his classic article "A Plea for Excuses," J. L. Austin showed that one cannot fully understand responsibility, ethical or legal, without adding the realm of excuses to that of normative rules that specify duties. "If ordinary language is to be our guide, it is to evade responsibility, or full responsibility, that we most often make excuses."[8]

No ethical or legal principle, whether very general or quite specific, applies to all persons in all contexts. There are difficulties with defining the scope of the obligation, identifying responsible parties, specifying overriding factors, and recognizing unusual contexts not meant to be covered by the principle. These problems are usually raised by the alleged violator claiming an excuse. Then some person or process must decide whether the excuse is sufficient to avoid the implication of responsibility or at least minimize the seriousness of the violation. In the law, this is a matter of defenses, and a lawyer who does not know the range of possible defenses would be incompetent. Should we also say of ethical systems and ethicists that if they do not deal with excuses, they are not competent?

A second reason to carefully consider excuses is that those that are used and accepted could indicate that the ethical standards themselves may need to be reformulated. When a general rule is regularly disobeyed and a justification is routinely offered and accepted for such violation, the rule loses its claim to validity.

Many excuses I have heard professionals or students use are broad enough to seriously undercut professional responsibility. They seemed to imply that an ethical system developed in the nineteenth and early twentieth century does not fit well the way we provide professional services in the late twentieth and twenty-first century.

A third problem highlighted by excuses would be recognized by lawyers as serious, but it is an even more serious problem for ethicists. If we have developed a satisfactory contemporary system for affixing professional ethical responsibility and a set of excuses that are available for preventing that system from being too rigid or all encompassing, who decides when it is appropriate to use an excuse? Lawyers have developed relatively objective social institutions, such as courts and juries, to answer such questions. In ethical systems, these are often matters for the actors themselves to decide. We understand the capacity of humans to rationalize or fool themselves on matters where their perceived self-interest is involved. This raises important questions about whether any system, ethical or otherwise, based on voluntary compliance can be effective.

A fourth issue raised by excuses is the degree of freedom or control that contemporary professionals have over their activities and whether they always have the opportunity or, as some might say, the luxury of acting ethically. A number of the ethical excuses discussed in Chapter 3 go to this question.

Unfortunately we do not often think clearly about excuses. In fact, we do not think much about them at all. This is curious because we all use excuses and hear them used toward us many times each day. Perhaps excuses are so much a part of the background of life that we have lost the ability to distinguish them from all the other audible clutter.

My formal training as a lawyer has produced two additional emphases to the discussions in this book. Although I am an academic lawyer, law itself is a practical and applied field, so one can never escape the questions of whether something matters in the real world and whether it works or not. Second, lawyers are much concerned with questions of borders, that is to say, appropriate areas of jurisdiction for various fields of law, of legal systems, and of law itself. There are serious questions about how law and ethics overlap. These jurisdictional questions are particularly difficult in professional ethics. One way of exploring the areas of overlap and where the boundaries should be drawn is to compare excuses in ethics and defenses in the law. This may help to illuminate problems in both fields.

This book is also an exploration of personal dilemmas I have been unable to satisfactorily resolve over a long lifetime. The discussion is an effort to explore and understand those issues better, rather than attempting to answer once and for all problems we must all live with and cannot ever completely overcome. That is why the tone will often be personal and the voice first person singular. On occasion, I use the first person plural not from any aspirations toward the royal "we," but because I hope this will be in some way a dialogue between each reader and me.

I believe strongly in the necessity for individuals to have a high set of ethical standards and to live by them. Everybody has several sets of morals, among them a personal code and another the one he uses to judge the actions of others. The moral code by which one evaluates his own actions should be more demanding than the one used to judge and condemn others. In practice, this tends to be reversed. We are often more tolerant of our own lapses than those of others around us. Do professionals claim a higher ethics than required of lay people, but tolerate in themselves a more lenient application than expected of those others?

While there ought to be a high level of personal ethics for each of us, there are social pressures and personal needs that seem to push us into unethical action against our own wishes. I have sometimes tolerated my own lapses, while I have criticized others for not meeting those same standards. Consequently I have paid a heavy price in that twentieth-century psychological purgatory, with high levels of guilt which cannot be forgiven because there is no confessional or forum where one can confess, discuss and ameliorate the problem, or make atonement.

The field of excuses, which is largely unexamined both in theory and in our common culture, is the battleground where the daily conflict between high ethical expectations and the pressures to cross the lines constantly takes place. The exploration of that psychological war zone for me and for others is in large part the purpose of this book.

NOTES

1. There is an interesting discussion of both the definition and the criteria of professionalism in Andrew Abbott, THE SYSTEM OF PROFESSIONS: AN ESSAY ON THE DIVISION OF EXPERT LABOR (Chicago: The University of Chicago Press, 1988), pp. 3–9.

2. WEBSTER'S NINTH COLLEGIATE DICTIONARY (Springfield, Mass.: Merriam-Webster, 1987), p. 307.

3. One example is the practice of the infamous New York City Law firm of Howe and Hummel during the nineteenth century. By alleging breach of promise of marriage by beautiful showgirls against wealthy admirers, they raised blackmail to such a lucrative activity that many states passed statutes outlawing this legal action as a result. See Richard H. Rovere, HOWE AND HUMMEL: THEIR TRUE AND SCANDALOUS HISTORY (New York: Farrar, Straus, 1947). No unethical activity by lawyers today could be worse than the work of this firm.

4. The assumption of perfect compliance on which most ethical theories are constructed avoids many of the real problems any effective system of applied ethics must deal with. See Michael Bales, "Ethical Theory in the Twenty-First Century," in Joseph P. DeMarco and Richard M. Fox, NEW DIRECTIONS IN ETHICS: THE CHALLENGE OF APPLIED ETHICS (New York and London: Routledge & Kegan Paul, 1986), pp. 257–258.

5. Banks McDowell, ETHICAL CONDUCT AND THE PROFESSIONAL'S DILEMMA: CHOOSING BETWEEN SERVICE AND SUCCESS (Westport, Conn.: Quorum Books, 1991).

6. See John Rawls, A THEORY OF JUSTICE (Cambridge, Mass.: Harvard University Press, 1972), pp. 8–9, where he says:

I consider primarily what I call strict compliance as opposed to partial compliance theory. . . . The latter studies the principles that govern how we are to deal with injustice. It comprises such topics as the theory of punishment, the doctrine of just war, and the justification of the various ways of opposing unjust regimes, ranging from civil disobedience and militant resistance to revolution and rebellion. Also included here are questions of compensatory justice and of weighing one form of institutional injustice against another. Obviously the problems of partial compliance theory are the pressing and urgent matters. These are the things that we are faced with in everyday life. The reason for beginning with ideal theory is that it provides, I believe, the only basis for the systematic grasp of these more pressing problems.

7. An example of legislative regulation of conflict of interest problems faced by professionals is 18 U.S.C.A. 207, a federal statute that makes it criminal for any former employee of the executive department or an independent federal agency to appear as an agent or attorney in any matter about which he or she was engaged as a governmental employee for any party other than the United States for a specified period of time. For a contemporary and thorough canvassing of federal ethics

statutes and violations of them, see Kathleen Clark, "Do We Have Enough Ethics in Government Yet?: An Answer from Fiduciary Theory," UNIVERSITY OF ILLINOIS LAW REVIEW (February 1996): 58–63.

8. J. L. Austin, "A Plea for Excuses," PHILOSOPHICAL PAPERS, 3d ed. (New York: Oxford University Press, 1979), p. 181.

2

Responsibility and Excuses

If the problems facing professionals are not ones of learning the expectations of professional ethics, but rather of complying with them, we need to
look closely at the excuses offered and, even more important, those that are
accepted for alleged lapses from ethical standards. As a preliminary matter
before we get to the typical excuses, I want to discuss several central questions. (a) What do we mean by saying that a professional is responsible? (b)
What is the function of excuses? (c) How do we describe successful or unsuccessful excuses? (d) Who decides whether an excuse works?

WHEN CAN WE SAY A PROFESSIONAL IS RESPONSIBLE?

In simple moral analysis, *responsibility* is the consequence of obligation
and the failure to comply, the conclusion of a syllogism in which the major
premise is the duty and the minor premise is the breach. In other words, it is
an inference or conclusion from the presence of other factors.

Responsibility is the major concern of most evaluative judgments of human action. If we think in causal terms about people, we must identify
which actor should be credited for some result we either approve or disap-
prove of. We then describe that person as the responsible party. Otherwise
we would have to label the occurrence as an accident, act of nature, or act of
God, which are conclusions egocentric human beings are reluctant to draw.
We may need to seriously reexamine the traditional assumption that we
ought to identify a responsible individual for most actions. We will consider that question in Chapter 7.

We locate responsibility not only to condemn, but also to praise. One of the most laudatory comments we make about a person is that she is responsible. This means she accepts her duties, carries them out completely and thoroughly, and willingly accepts the consequences of her actions. Just as saying that a person is responsible is great praise, declaring her irresponsible is serious condemnation. It seems almost a character flaw, meaning she is unreliable, untrustworthy, someone who cannot be counted on when difficulties arise.

Responsibility must be accepted before one acts or at the very least while acting and before one knows what the consequences will be. There is always risk of condemnation, but also the possibility of reward or praise. Taking credit after the consequences are known if they are favorable and avoiding it if the consequences are unfavorable is a common human reaction, but one that is the antithesis of taking responsibility.

An important distinction is between responsibility imposed from the outside and that which is voluntarily accepted by the actor. Legal responsibility is imposed by government officials. What might be called social responsibility is imposed by family, friends, and peers. Responsibility that is self-imposed is an important aspect in defining the realm of the ethical.

Responsibility for wrongful actions is difficult for most people to accept. Children instinctively avoid it by denying the reality of wrongdoing, by lying, or by giving excuses, whether persuasive or not. This conduct often continues past childhood. Being held responsible for wrongful or damaging acts leads to unpleasantness, and there is a powerful urge to defend against or to try to evade such consequences. As long as excuses work, one is not held responsible. An important mark of maturity or adulthood is the willingness to accept responsibility. Ethics requires the acceptance of responsibility, particularly when there is no doubt about its appropriateness in the particular context. The signal that one has accepted responsibility is the offering of an apology, rather than the giving of an excuse. In some non-Western cultures, it is very common to offer an apology and that is often accepted as all that is necessary. The more usual response in western culture is to try to avoid responsibility by giving an excuse.

One constantly hears public complaints today that people are no longer responsible. This is often directed toward poor people on welfare, toward some disfavored ethnic or racial groups, or toward young people by parents or teachers. Those who call for acceptance of responsibility mean this criticism for others, not for themselves. Such critics are not noticeably more reticent about using excuses to avoid having to take responsibility themselves.

What does the ascription of responsibility entail in ethics? We know that legal responsibility is almost always followed by some sanction, such as the requirement of paying compensation to victims, payment of a fine, imprisonment, or, in the most extreme cases, capital punishment. In ethics, accepting responsibility means accepting blame for unethical actions and feeling remorse or guilt. Remorse and guilt are powerful forces and can create substantial pain.

For the actor or professional who is accused of acting unethically, we should distinguish conscious and unconscious levels of awareness. If the actor produces an excuse that he finds acceptable at a conscious level, but still feels guilt, he has unconsciously accepted responsibility. The excuse, which appears to work at a conscious level, has not worked at a deeper level of consciousness.

The Ethical Obligation

One never uses the words or claims that we label excuses, justifications, defenses, or alibis unless a putative duty exists that the obligor has not complied with. So the first issue in ascribing responsibility is to determine whether such a duty is present. That has been the primary concern of most ethical analysis and teaching.

There must be a normative *duty* or obligation to act in some way; that is, one ought to do something or refrain from doing something.[1] This creates the ethical obligation. Such a duty can arise from a variety of sources: personal convictions, conscience, the expectations of peers, social conventions about right and wrong actions, and formal statements of moral duties.

From among these sources, formal statements and social conventions will be of continuing importance in this discussion. For professionals, the formal statement is the code of ethics developed by each profession, coupled with whatever glosses are placed on them by the professional association and their ethics committees. There are, in addition to formal codes, social conventions about proper and improper actions, which are more complex, less universal, and tend to operate at a less conscious level. These are the informal moral codes at work in the professions, only imperfectly reflected in the formal codes.

While normative duties are varied and may be legal, ethical, religious, social, or personal, the important qualifier for us is the adjective ethical. Which of the many duties we are subject to should be thought of as ethical and within that subcategory of duties, which should be considered as professional ethical obligations? This question will be considered in Chapter 4 in detail.

We could rest the duty element solely on those obligations created or at least authenticated by the formal professional codes of ethics. I prefer at this stage to keep the sources of ethical obligation broader. Professionals are not just professionals, but human beings, responding not only to professional ethics, but also to all the ethical imperatives placed on individuals. A broader recognition of sources of duty keeps open the theoretical, and often real, possibility of conflicts between professional duties and other obligations. An ongoing conflict for professionals arises because there are informal codes of behavior that are not always consistent with the formal code. An advantage of looking at professional conduct through the lens of excuses is that these may point to where the formal codes are unrealistic, ignored, or too limited. That critical opportunity would be diminished or largely lost if we used as a starting basis only the formal professional codes of ethics themselves.

Lying behind the codes and impinging on professionals as well as ordinary people are cultural notions about right and wrong. Few people deny that such ethical precepts exist or that they are obligatory. Despite cultural, ethnic, and religious diversity, there is a surprising agreement about what in general those obligations are. That agreement is the product of a common human nature and a shared culture.

Those cultural notions of right and wrong we learn as children also contain the notion of special duties in close relationships, such as exist between family members or close friends. The virtue of loyalty requires us to recognize these special claims unless we were to take the absurd position that we owe loyalty in equal proportions to every institution and every person. People understand naturally the concept of fiduciary relationships, such as guardian and ward, godparent and godchild, mentor and apprentice. The professional and client relationship on which professional ethics is built is just another such relationship.

In identifying whether there is an ethical duty in a particular context, the most reliable guide is not the formal code. Nor is it conduct. It is dangerous to infer a norm from conduct. We often act in ways we should not. A better indicator of a real and functioning norm is a feeling of guilt for not complying, manifested by the felt need to give an excuse. Of course, guilt is not a perfect indicator of improper action, since others may manipulate us into feeling guilty when we should not.

One excuse always logically possible is that there are no binding ethical obligations, the analogy in ethics to the anarchist in politics. It is, however, much more common to deny the existence of the particular norm at issue. Beyond the broad claim that there are no ethical obligations at all, any other excuse is a tacit admission of the binding force of the ethical system and usually of the ethical norm or obligation in question.

Before leaving this introduction to ethical obligation, I want to identify two analytical distinctions used throughout the book. They were developed by Wesley Hohfeld, a law professor who early in the twentieth century developed a system to help lawyers think clearly.[2] He felt all legal rules defined relationships, and there were only four fundamental relationships, out of which more complex relationships were built, much as a molecule is built of atoms. Much confusion occurred, he thought, because lawyers use the same term interchangeably to describe quite different relationships, the best example of this confusing multiple uses being "right." Hohfeld thought his distinctions made for much clearer thought and analysis in law, and I think they do in ethics as well.

For Hohfeld, "duty" was always the correlative of "right," and unless some identifiable person had a claim or "right," there was no duty. A host of problems and much confused thinking in professional ethics arise from failure to keep this idea clearly in mind. First, one must identify to whom the professional's duty is owed. If she owes competing duties at the same time and place to different people, she must decide which is the overriding or more compelling duty.

A simplistic view of professional ethics says there is no problem because the overriding duty is always owed to the client. This is the product of thinking only in terms of the simple autonomous professional–single client model. The professional has many clients; hence the often unavoidable conflicts of duty. The professional also owes duties to fellow professionals, to family and friends, and often to members of the public with whom he comes into contact in the course of his professional activity.[3] If we think the choice problem is simple and the professional always owes the primary duty to the client, we have defined out of our consciousness some of the most difficult ethical problems professionals face.

Another useful distinction drawn by Hohfeld is the relationship he defined as "privilege–no right." Privilege is the area of freedom where we can act; however, we choose without anyone else having the "right" to complain about what we do. Professional ethics is a continuing battleground about the boundary lines between these two types of relationships. Professionals want their activity to come primarily inside the realm of privilege; that is, they stake out a large claim of professional autonomy. That is a claim with which I have much sympathy. However, when one accepts that a duty is owed to someone else, whether client, fellow professional, or spouse, which is, to say, that person has a right or a claim that we act in a certain way, we are no longer privileged to act as we wish, but only as we must. Even if there are conflicting claims, we are obligated to honor the strongest of the claims. There is no privilege to choose a weaker claim or to ignore all the claims.

Autonomy is important to professionals who believe that they do and should enjoy wide freedom in practicing their profession and utilizing their expertise. Some excuses discussed in the next chapter are based on the notion that in the particular context the professional in fact had no such autonomy and thus should not be ethically responsible.

Autonomy is an important condition not just for professionals, but for all people. The ethical choice has to be a free choice; that is, the actor could have acted in more than one way and the options are not morally indifferent.[4] One way of acting has to be better than the other, or stated in ethical terms, one course of action is good and the other bad. If both courses of action are equally good, there is no problem of ethical choice. And if the actor can act in only one way, it makes no sense to worry about whether that action should be considered ethical or unethical. A major reason for labeling something good or bad is to influence choice.

The Ethical Breach

A *breach* is action that goes against the requirements of the norm. It is action that is regarded as abnormal or wrong. This constitutes the second element in the fixing of ethical responsibility. Breach is a shorthand way of saying that the particular action of the professional does not comply with the appropriate ethical standard. Rule-obeying behavior is generally not noticed or is taken for granted, that is, accepted as normal—as what should occur.[5]

This creates a serious problem of observational bias. Because we take the normal for granted and tend to stress the abnormal, we may exaggerate the degree of criminality or unethical action in our world because we do not clearly notice and consciously record the proportion of human activity that is normal and ethical. This caution needs to be kept in mind when deciding whether to accept the introductory assumption of this book, which is, that we face an ethical crisis.

Small children often deny moral breaches even in the face of overwhelming evidence that they did it. Adults are less likely to deny an obvious breach, but more likely to try to transfer the responsibility to someone else. It is not unknown, of course, for children to use this same technique, claiming, "My brother did it" or "The dog did it." One of the common professional excuses discussed in the next chapter is the claim that someone else actually did the action or was responsible for whatever injury occurred.

Another possible claim about this element that can be made by someone accused of unethical activity is to assert that the action and any resulting damage was insignificant or trivial and so should not be considered an ethical breach by anyone. It is hard to know whether one should treat this as an excuse or as part of the definition of what constitutes a breach. In other words, the definition could require that a breach must be substantial.

Auxiliary Concepts

In addition to the central concepts of duty, breach, and responsibility that are necessary to understand the role of excuses, there are three others that can be relevant. Their importance is not so much in explaining how excuses work, but rather in answering questions that will arise in the rest of the book. First, when is an ethical violation so serious that it calls for an excuse to be made? Second, when there is more than one candidate for the role of responsible party, how do we select the one to be held responsible? Finally, when there has been a serious violation of a norm that is both legal and ethical, how do we assign it to the appropriate realm?

The first auxiliary concept is *damage*. Damage goes to the seriousness of the injury and establishes a threshold. That threshold must be such that a victim is likely to complain and the actor feels a necessity to produce an excuse. Must an unethical act produce some harm to another before it should be considered unethical? As a first-year law student, I was surprised to learn that traditional legal analysis required that an "illegal" act produce harm before it was actionable. For example, a person is often negligent in driving his automobile, either exceeding the speed limit or driving recklessly, but she has not committed a tort, an illegal act, unless somebody is injured by her carelessness. Should the same analysis be used in practical ethics?[6]

The importance of damage as an element in understanding excuses is not so dependent on whether or not one adopts a consequentialist theory, as it is on three practical considerations.

The first reason is essentially administrative. We frequently act in ways that violate prudent, rational, or moral notions, but neither we nor others take such action seriously until it produces harm. The existence of damage is our way of separating trivial from serious matters.

Second, excuses need not be given until someone complains. Excuses are essentially a part of the interpersonal aspect of immoral activity. The other person, usually the victim, would seldom raise the issue of unethical action unless he has been harmed.

Finally, in the practical world, we analyze these issues in reverse form. Responsibility is signaled by the fact we must pay a price, that is, the imposition of some sanction such as physical punishment, monetary fines, or blame. That would normally occur only when we have done some harm to another. We cannot impose the sanction on someone for damage until we are sure he is the one who really caused the injury, so what I have called "auxiliary concepts" are useful to the whole enterprise of determining responsibility, which gives rise to the need for excuses.

Related to this issue of the importance of damage in calling forth the need for excuses and then using excuses as a key to unethical behavior is the question of what kinds of unsatisfactory behavior by professionals should be labeled unethical. When the professional establishes a relationship of trust with a client and then produces an unsatisfactory result, the client will feel he has been mistreated and will make a claim of incompetence or unethical behavior. The explanation given by the professional will be regarded as an excuse and thus falls within the analysis of this book.

There must be *causation*, some connection between the breach of the duty and damage to create legal liability. Should we not say the same of ethical misconduct? It is implicit in the analysis, but often not explicit. Causation becomes an important element only if damage occurs and one is trying to connect that to a responsible actor.

Finally there is the element of *sanction*. When detected, illegal activity is almost invariably followed by the imposition of some unpleasant consequence. Should we say the same of unethical activity? Is blame or the existence of guilt the functional equivalent of a sanction? Certainly blame from others is unpleasant and is a consequence we want to avoid just as we want to avoid the effects of legal sanctions. Guilt is a more interesting puzzle. Like blame, it is also an unpleasant sensation and presumably we wish to avoid pain so the assumption is that we will tend to live our lives in ways that minimize the degree of guilt we feel. It is, however, internal and is not imposed from the outside, so to deal with it as a sanction, we may be forced into the metaphor of the split personality with one part (the superego?) imposing the guilt and another part (the ego?) suffering.

How are these elements related and used in a full-blown analysis of ethical responsibility? We might think we look for an ethical duty, find if there has been a breach, ask if damage was caused by the breach to a victim, and then decide whether there is a connection between the breach and that damage. Responsibility would then be a consequence of finding that all these elements were present. This describes an analytical or theoretical way of talking about responsibility, which is helpful in understanding the elements or concepts involved. Actually this process is almost totally reversed in ordinary human transactions.

What is the trigger for ethical analysis of our daily actions? Most often it is a claim by a victim, an observer, or a supervisor that a person has acted unethically. In an internal analysis, the trigger may be the fear someone might make such a claim. It is only then that excuses are trotted out and one works backward through the chain of elements. A claim of unethical activity is unlikely to be made until there has been harm. The claim comes only after someone has been identified as the causal agent. The excuse raises the question of whether there was a duty and a breach by the actor. This process of evaluating action after the fact is often described as hindsight knowledge or "Monday morning quarterbacking" and often carries a connotation of unfairness about evaluating an activity after the event. Practically, however, that is the only time it is possible to evaluate an actual event, rather than speculate about probabilities or possibilities, which may not even occur.

One way of excusing the breach and thus evading responsibility is to deny the existence of any one of these elements. We might say that there was no duty, that our acts did not breach a duty, that no damage was done, or that our breach did not cause the damage. There are, however, ethical excuses, as we will see in Chapter 3, and legal defenses, as discussed in Chapter 5, which accept that all of these conceptual elements are present and still contend the actor is not responsible.

WHAT ARE THE FUNCTIONS OF EXCUSES?

The excuse intervenes between the breach and the conclusion of responsibility. It is usually a relational act by which a wrongdoer explains himself to another and seeks to avoid the ascription of responsibility. The actor may be excusing himself to himself, engaging in an internal dialogue trying to escape guilt. This could be thought of analytically as a relational act between different parts of the personality. In order to escape responsibility, he must offer some reason why the norm did not apply or that he should not be seen as violating it.

Excuses are Janus-faced. They can be the means by which a "responsible" person avoids the social or personal consequences of improper actions. However, they are also the means by which the rigidity of universal and perfectionist normative systems can be given flexibility and adapted to complex or unusual individual situations. In this latter type of function, excuses are not avoidance of responsibility, but a tool of adaptability and of critical evaluation. In discussing the problem of adapting moral positions and justifications to the incredible variety of contexts in which human beings act, Stuart Hampshire said:

> The parallel with language is useful. It has so far proved impossible to design a translating machine which takes account of the indefinite variety of contexts, linguistic and external, in which a given form of words is used; and normally the contexts affect the sense. However elaborate the programme built into the machine, it is apt to fall short, if only because of the sheer unpredictable variety of contexts encountered. The variety is not only humanly unpredictable but humanly unimaginable. Yet a person translating immediately sees the recurring form of words against the background of a different context and then intuitively makes the required adjustment to the sense. A person is a complex mechanism naturally designed over a long evolutionary period to make such adjustments.[7]

Excuses are often the way an actor accused of acting unethically contends that the context in which the claim is made is different from the set of paradigm cases the rule was intended to cover, so it is inappropriate to hold him morally responsible for violating the rule. Given the abstract and almost universal form of most ethical rules and the way we analyze moral issues, that issue of overinclusiveness cannot be raised directly but must be broached indirectly through the use of an excuse.

This process of excusing questionable behavior may be totally internal; that is, the professional can know she has an ethical duty and that she has probably violated that duty. She then proposes to herself an excuse explaining the way she acted and if the excuse seems persuasive, she does not feel she must assume any responsibility.

The process can be totally external. The duty will be imposed by the code of professional ethics or admonitions of other professionals. Some victim, often a client, will claim to have been harmed by the violation of an ethical principle. There might then be a formal hearing by an ethics committee of the professional association where the accused professional will offer an excuse and the committee will decide whether the excuse is persuasive or not and thus find the professional either responsible or not.

Whether the procedure is wholly internal, wholly external, or a mix of the two, excuses function the same way, sometimes as a means of avoiding responsibility, other times as a means of making the ascription of responsibility better adapted to context and complexity.

HOW DO WE DESIGNATE SUCCESSFUL OR UNSUCCESSFUL EXCUSES?

The word "excuse" carries different meanings. One meaning, suggested by the word "alibi," is an attempt to *avoid responsibility* legitimately placed on the actor. Another meaning is a justification,[8] a persuasive reason, for being excepted from an otherwise applicable ethical obligation. "Excuse" may also refer to an *explanation* as to why the unethical conduct occurred. Such explanations are useful if one wants to change conduct.[9]

In order to avoid confusion in the following discussion, I use "excuse" as the generic term. Since an excuse may be either a good or a bad one, the term carries no value connotation. It serves only the function of saying that a claimed duty does not apply to an actor so that his acts are not a breach and therefore he ought not to bear any responsibility for the actions. When discussing a valid excuse, I will call it a "justification," or sometimes, a "persuasive excuse." This means that even if there was a duty and the actor breached that duty, there is some reason why moral responsibility should not be attributed to him.[10]

When describing an unpersuasive or invalid excuse, I will use the term "alibi." The common usage of "alibi" is a claim that the alleged actor was not present at the time and place of the action so he could not be responsible. Since it usually carries a connotation of being unpersuasive, if not untrue, I adopt a wider usage of the term to cover all unpersuasive excuses. In the next chapter, I discuss many common excuses offered by professionals, some of which in the right context are genuine justifications, but in other situations would be alibis.

If I am talking about a reason merely given by the actor to make clear why he acted the way he did, I will call it an "explanation." If the actor decides whether the excuse is persuasive enough to avoid responsibility, the "explanation" will also serve as a justification, but if others make the judgment about the excuse's validity, "explanation" is merely the actor's way of viewing the situation.

Another important linguistic distinction signals the difference between legal and ethical systems. "Excuse" is the appropriate term when discussing ethical obligations. In reference to legal obligations, one speaks of "defenses."

WHO DECIDES WHETHER AN EXCUSE IS SATISFACTORY?

A significant difference between the normative systems of law and of ethics is that the legal system has developed a means by which the validity of an excuse can be determined "objectively." This process is the trial during which a judge and/or jury will hear the reasons given by the actor for not complying with the law and will decide whether they constitute a persuasive defense. Even if no trial is held, the defendant must be prepared for such an eventuality. Thus his defenses must not merely be persuasive to himself, but appear likely to persuade judges and jurors. The decision by the court would, of course, not be merely a personal decision, but constrained by a centuries-long development of rules, standards, and distinctions that the judge and jury are supposed to take account of. No such procedure exists in ethical systems. The closest analog for professionals would be the opinion of peers or possible victims who may indicate whether they find the excuse persuasive or not.

For practical ethics, the actor is the most important judge of whether an excuse is valid. If he feels there is a justification for not obeying an ethical norm, he is free to act in accordance with his perceived self-interest. This makes ethics largely a system of voluntary compliance. Of course, others, such as clients, victims, bystanders, or fellow professionals, may evaluate the excuse and they could well decide that it was not valid. If they do not inform the actor of their feelings, which is a strong possibility in our culture where an important informal moral maxim is "mind your own business," or if the actor does not care about their opinion, there is no constraint on acting in an unethical fashion. As long as an excuse exists that the actor can persuade himself or herself is a valid justification, ethical systems will have little bite in controlling action. This freedom to be indifferent to ethical systems has been exacerbated in modern urban life with the breakup of close communities and tight family structure.

We will return to this problem, which is the primary focus of this book, in Chapter 9.

NOTES

1. For a valuable discussion of the various meanings of "ought" or "obligation" and the dangers of restricting those to rule-based duties, see Joel Feinberg, DOING AND DESERVING: ESSAYS IN THE THEORY OF RESPONSIBILITY (Princeton: Princeton University Press, 1970), pp. 3–9.

2. Wesley N. Hohfeld, FUNDAMENTAL LEGAL CONCEPTIONS (New Haven: Yale University Press, 1919). An abbreviated introduction to Hohfeldian

analysis appears in Arthur L. Corbin, "Legal Analysis and Terminology," 29 YALE LAW JOURNAL (1919): 163–173.

3. An example of this last conflict familiar to lawyers is the question of whether a defendant's attorney in a rape case owes any duties to the victim. This issue is raised by the practice of defense lawyers, who are trying to protect their client, viciously attacking the victim's reputation and veracity, a process so debilitating that many victims refuse to complain rather than face that prospect.

4. Isaiah Berlin in the introduction to his FOUR ESSAYS ON LIBERTY (London, Oxford University Press, 1969), pp. xi–xv, argues persuasively that ethical choices entailing the ascription of responsibility must be free in this sense.

5. There is an interesting question about conduct, which as a matter of politics or rebelliousness violates contemporary norms of customary action. Much creative activity may have this quality. Should one think of this as an excuse or should we define our norms as creating an exception for such activity? A major issue in political theory is how much value should be given to obedient and conforming behavior and what value to iconoclastic and questioning activity against society's norms.

6. For readers trained in moral philosophy, I want to clarify that "damage" is not used in the sense of consequences in utilitarian theory, but the way a lawyer uses the term. The focus is on an identifiable and quantifiable injury done to a person who complains and who insists that justice requires some form of recompense. For the lawyer, this normally means money damages. In ethical systems, it would require acceptance of blame, apologies, or atonement.

7. Stuart Hampshire, "Public and Private Morality," in PUBLIC AND PRIVATE MORALITY, Stuart Hampshire, ed. (Cambridge: Cambridge University Press, 1978), p. 31.

8. The classic analysis of excuses is J. L. Austin, "A Plea for Excuses," PHILOSOPHICAL PAPERS, 3d ed. (New York: Oxford University Press, 1979). Austin gives justification and excuse a different meaning than I do. When an actor admits that she acted in a certain way, but claims it was a good thing is what he means by justification. In contrast, the situation when the actor admits that she acted in a wrong way, but offers an explanation in order to partly or totally escape responsibility is what he means by excuse. I am interested in how one distinguishes between persuasive and unpersuasive excuses. The person to be persuaded may be an objective observer, a professional or legal institution, or the actor herself.

Criminal law theorists also often distinguish justifications from excuses. See George P. Fletcher, RETHINKING CRIMINAL LAW (Boston: Little, Brown and Company, 1978), pp. 759–762. The practical reason for this distinction is that justified conduct would not allow the victim to act in self-defense whereas a mere excuse would. Although that problem can on occasion be a serious one for legal systems, it is not for ethical analysis. The distinction I am concerned with is the difference between those excuses that successfully avoid responsibility by an actor and those which do not.

9. I do not distinguish here between a completely persuasive excuse, a partial excuse, and a totally invalid excuse. These distinctions, which control the degree of responsibility an actor has, fall largely outside the focus and analysis of this chapter.

10. As indicated in Note 8 above, many moral philosophers and legal theorists insist on a difference between justification and excuse, a distinction I will not use. For them, justification is an explanation why the action did not violate a moral duty. An excuse admits there was a violation of moral duty, but is an explanation as to why moral responsibility in part or in full should not fall on the actor. That analysis assumes that the primary issue before the theorist is whether there was a moral duty or not and the decision is being made by an objective observer. My view is that in the practical world, the issue is always whether the actor is responsible or not for a questionable action and that decision is usually being made by the actor or someone affected by the action. "Justification" in ordinary language means a persuasive explanation as to why responsibility is not applicable. Such a broad meaning is given by the *Oxford English Dictionary*: "The action of justifying or showing something to be just, right, or proper; vindication of oneself or another; exculpation . . . b. That which justifies; a justifying circumstance; an apology, a defense" (THE COMPACT EDITION OF THE OXFORD ENGLISH DICTIONARY) [New York: Oxford University Press, 1971], p. 1524). For purposes of my analysis, justification and persuasive excuse are synonymous and I shall so use them.

3

Ethical Excuses

The important excuses one hears, and often uses, in professional practice fall into seven groups. The actual excuses given are more complex, detailed, and varied, depending on the particular actors and the contexts in which they are operating. In order to understand the problems created by such excuses, it is only necessary to analyze the common forms that professionals offer for questionable activity.

When discussing ethical excuses, as contrasted with legal defenses, I am less concerned with what might be called mitigating excuses, those intended not to avoid, but to minimize, responsibility. It is a curious and, from an ethical perspective, important feature of humans that we prefer to be characterized as incompetent, careless, or inattentive rather than as deliberately or consciously evil. The degree of blame seems to be less from careless or incompetent actions than from intentionally unethical activity. Professionals, however, are not likely to give mitigating excuses when engaged in professional activity. Such excuses raise serious questions about their competence. A professional is not supposed to be inattentive or incompetent or careless when dealing with the affairs of his client. Such excuses raise doubts about whether he is entitled to continue to act as a professional.

The consequence of acting unethically is to incur blame or guilt, but blame and guilt are hard to apportion between total and partial. One has either acted unethically or not and is blamed or not. In contrast, the law has a whole range of graduated sanctions that it can impose. If the court cannot be persuaded there is a complete defense, there are questions about how plausible the defense is and how much responsibility the defendant has incurred because those doubts may affect the type and amount of sanction imposed. The seven groups of excuses, which follow, may be persuasive excuses or mere alibis, depending on the context. At the end of the chapter, I will discuss three additional excuses used on occasion by professionals that are seldom, if ever, persuasive.

THE CLAIM OF IGNORANCE

One excuse often used is "I did not know what the ethical requirements were." While this is not precisely a claim that there was no duty, it argues implicitly that only those duties known to the actor ought to be obligatory. The short answer to that contention is that a professional should know the ethical requirements.

Such an excuse may be sincere, particularly among older professionals who were not required to take courses in professional ethics. Some ethical requirements are counterintuitive; such as the rigid requirement of confidentiality placed on lawyers, priests, and perhaps doctors,[1] even if the information in question is about harm being done to third parties.

Required ethics courses undercut the legitimacy and persuasiveness of the excuse of ignorance. Any system of regulatory standards that people must or ought to obey has to reject this claim of ignorance. "Ignorance of the law is no excuse," and if professional ethics is not just law, but ethics, ignorance of ethics should fare little better.

There are two genuine problems with the assumption that a person knows an ethical (or legal) duty in sufficient detail to always comply. One is the question of penumbra or periphery. All rules cover an area with fuzzy edges. There may be disagreement about whether a particular case on the boundary comes within a rule. The other problem is the degree of abstractness. Most ethical rules or principles are general and fairly abstract. The application of the standard to a particular context requires becoming specific. The legal system has developed a procedure, the trial, to resolve disagreements about fringe cases and the application of rules to particular contexts. Ethical systems have no analogous procedure, although some professional organizations have created ethics committees, one of whose functions is to answer questions about areas of uncertainty. If a professional is aware of a moral rule and that it might apply to a situation where she is acting, she has a responsibility to make sure that it does not apply to her actions. She cannot use the excuse that she thought her action was outside the fringe or did not know whether the rule fitted the particular context without some reasonable attempt to answer those questions.

There is a more sophisticated version of this excuse, which may appear more persuasive. Often people act immorally because they are not even aware that a particular context raises ethical issues.[2] Moral issues often pose difficult problems of choice and require changing conduct in ways that require the person to sacrifice other important goals. As long as one is unaware of moral issues, life is simpler and easier. The mere recognition of problems does not lead to their solution. Ignoring them does not either, but at least for a time one can perform in blissful ignorance.

Most professionals would say they are faced with a professional ethical dilemma a few times a month. My perception is that they are faced with moral issues many times every day. Underlying their claim of ignorance is the reality that they have not been taught to recognize all the moral questions before them. If parents, teachers, and friends avoid public discussion of moral problems, which is our cultural practice in general, then young people are not made sensitive to moral issues, nor do they learn to recognize them in the real world they inhabit. Are people who have been raised in that amoral way entitled to be unaware of ethical issues in their professional practice? Remember my comment in the preface that most of my students that I taught over a forty-year period were indifferent to issues of morality or ethics. Is not the recognition of moral problems a responsibility of being a professional, or of being a human? One can blame parents and teachers for not fulfilling an ethical duty by better preparing their charges to know about and deal with moral difficulties,[3] but that blame does not excuse the responsible actor.

Here I add an important qualification. While professionals are constantly faced with moral issues, it may not be practical to keep them always in the front of one's mind. Worrying about every ethical problem, however minor, and then struggling to find a proper solution may incapacitate the professional from performing the technical side of his obligations. A balance must be sought between sufficient awareness to recognize and deal with major ethical problems faced by the professional and the time necessary to concentrate on the technical problems he is being hired to solve. That is an issue of balance that professional ethical instruction and theory ought to confront openly and prepare professionals for.

To the extent this excuse of ignorance is sincere and widespread, increased instruction about ethical responsibilities designed to make practitioners aware of the frequency and types of moral problems they face is the appropriate response. Given the rapidly changing world of professional practice, this needs to be done both in professional school and in continuing-education programs.

THE TRANSFER OF RESPONSIBILITY

Perhaps the most common excuse is that a particular ethical breach was not the agent's responsibility, but someone else's. Much ethical analysis is built on a two-person model, the autonomous professional and the client. In such a simple model, it is difficult for a professional to evade responsibility for damage that her professional activities have caused a client. That model misses the reality of contemporary professional practice. Christopher Lasch observed:

> The prevalent mode of social interaction today is antagonistic cooperation (as David Riesman called it in *The Lonely Crowd*), in which a cult of teamwork conceals the struggle for survival within bureaucratic organizations.[4]

Most professional practice today is in large groups—law firms, accounting firms, or medical clinics and hospitals—that are bureaucratic in style and organization, and where professionals both compete and cooperate with each other. There are usually superiors, rivals for promotion, other members of the team, junior professionals, or staff who can be blamed for ethical lapses.[5]

From childhood on, it seems almost instinctive to pass blame to someone else. Harry Truman's famous statement "The buck stops here" is so striking because it seems an unusual assumption of responsibility for a contemporary person to take. A more representative figure is Ross Thomas's fictional con man, Otherguy Overby. The nickname "Otherguy" came from his often used and almost always successful excuse, "The other guy did it."[6]

Not only are specialized professional groups the dominant mode of practice today, but elite professionals who like to view themselves as autonomous are increasingly integrated into large corporate organizations.[7] Major corporations, private or governmental, have legal departments, medical clinics, accounting departments, engineering departments, and so forth. Blame can often be transferred onto other types of professionals.[8] This is not always a conscious evasion of responsibility. It may in fact be difficult to determine individual responsibility for ethical lapses in complex professional operations.

The contrast between the professional as individual autonomous practitioner and as a member of a large professional organization or a corporation raises another issue. It is the transfer of responsibility from a totally autonomous individual to that of a role player. In a slightly different context, when analyzing the problems of the holder of a public office, Thomas Nagel has perceptively posed the problem:

> There is, I think, a problem about the moral effects of public roles and offices. Certainly they have a profound effect on the behavior of the individuals who fill them, an effect partly restrictive but significantly liberating. Sometimes they confer great power, but even where they do not, as in the case of an infantryman or police interrogator, they can produce a feeling of moral insulation that has strong attractions. The combination of special requirements and release from some

of the usual restrictions, the ability to say that one is only following orders or doing one's job or meeting one's responsibilities, the sense that one is the agent of vast impersonal forces or the servant of institutions larger than any individual—all these ideas form a heady and sometimes corrupting brew.[9]

The distinction between public and private is ceasing to be as significant as that between individual and group or between small and large. Those professionals who are embedded in large bureaucratic organizations are akin to holders of public office. They can feel it is the organization and the organization's interests that set agendas and control action, so that individual moral choice is narrowed and unimportant. We will return to this issue in Chapter 7.

An individualist ethic, which permits the transfer of responsibility around the ring of participants in group activity, poses two difficult problems. The first is how to develop some method of fixing responsibility for a team activity onto a particular member, perhaps because he was the director of the team or else was the actor who was most closely connected causally to injuries caused a client. The legal system, which has faced this problem for decades, if not centuries, has developed theories of absolute, or nonfault liability, as a way to avoid this worrisome problem.[10]

The second issue is that of collective responsibility or guilt. This is an old, but increasingly important problem in ethics. There may be different degrees of unethical conduct. Not only the most causally significant actor bears ethical responsibility. The members of a team or group operating in supporting roles who merely observe the unethical activity of some member and then do not take whatever action is available to prevent the activity must bear some ethical responsibility for the result. This has been most discussed in connection with the responsibility of the German people for the Holocaust, but it is an issue that must be faced in any group or professional activity where some actors are unethical. Others cannot turn their heads away and disavow responsibility.

This process of group responsibility can lead to the practice familiar to most of us who were at any time in the military, where the entire platoon will be punished for the wrongful act of one soldier who cannot be identified by the sergeant. The expectation, which in my experience did not happen, was that the group would identify or know the culprit and punish him or her so the transgression will not occur again.[11] The practice leads ironically to a kind of team solidarity where every member will take the punishment rather than identify the culprit.

THE OVERRIDING OBLIGATION

In the real world, not the clean world of much ethical theory, professionals have multiple relationships, including large numbers of clients. This gives rise to the most difficult of all ethical obligations, to avoid conflicts of interest. There constantly are tough choices to be made among competing duties. While such problems are particularly acute for lawyers, politicians, accountants, and financial advisors, they exist for any professional offering services to many clients.

All professionals have a multiplicity of relationships, not only among clients, but with fellow professionals, family members, friends, and less tangible interests to consider, such as the public, the community, the working group, and so on. Finally, there are the interests of the professional herself. Professional ethics has tended to focus on the defining relationship of the professional, that with the client, and require her to avoid conflicts between the obligations owed various clients. The view seems to be that the professional should avoid not only conflicts, but the appearance of conflict as well. That is, frankly, an unachievable goal.

If a professional owes obligations that run to two or more persons and because of time and space limitations only one of the obligations can be fulfilled, a choice must be made. The claimant whose right to performance was not fulfilled will complain. The standard excuse given is that failure to perform was because an obligation owed to someone else was more compelling or important.

There are two quite different ethical issues here. One is the question of assuming more obligations than the professional can satisfactorily perform. One could say the professional should have assumed only one or a limited set of obligations. That attitude underlies much of our thinking about conflict-of-interest situations. In the complex world we live in, such a solution is not generally achievable. The professional who is essentially selling her time in blocks cannot always find a single client who will use the entire time or can plan her time so that the needs of multiple clients will not overlap and conflict.

If there are two different obligations, only one of which can be performed, the next ethical problem is whether the choice was made in a defensible manner, selecting the most demanding obligation to perform while minimizing damage to the client whose rights were not fulfilled. Professional ethics should concentrate more on developing guidelines as to how such choices should be made.

The most stringent rules on avoiding conflicts of interest apply to professionals in public office, most notably judges. Thomas Nagel discusses the issue as it relates to public office:

> In a rigidly defined role like that of a soldier or judge or prison guard, only a very restricted set of considerations is supposed to bear on what one decides to do, and nearly all general considerations are excluded. With less definition, other public offices limit their occupants to certain considerations and free them from others, such as the

good of mankind. Public figures even say and believe that they are obliged to consider only the national or state interest in arriving at their decision as if it would be a breach of responsibility for them to consider anything else.[12]

Nagel rejects this as too absolute a view of the obligations of a public role. One could apply the same conclusion to professional roles. When one rejects the absoluteness of each particular professional obligation, the number of obligations that must be considered in making choices is multiplied. Priority problems become ever more troublesome. The difficulties are created not by ethical expectations, but by the complex relationships of modern life.

The conflict-of-interest rules arise out of a simplistic and extreme notion of the duty of loyalty. Professional ethics proclaim that the professional owes a duty of fidelity to a client and nothing ought to supersede that. This is why a professional should avoid conflicts of interest. Only a few examples will show how pervasive these problems are and how impossible it is to avoid conflicts.

A common problem is an issue facing pediatricians, who owe a duty to the parent and to the child. In the case of suspected child abuse, does the duty to the child supersede the duty to the parent, who incidentally chose the doctor and is paying the fees, or at least the parent's insurer is? The doctor who breaches her loyalty to the parent by reporting to the authorities will claim the excuse of an overriding obligation, the welfare of the child. Of course, this choice of protecting the child has had to be imposed on many doctors by legislation or administrative regulation. A good many physicians were making the choice the other way. One complicating factor is that a pediatrician's failure to maintain confidentiality will prevent many parents at risk from consulting professionals when matters are still manageable and thus drive serious social and personal problems underground where they are more difficult to detect or treat.

Another unavoidable conflict is between professional obligations and obligations owed to families. An example has occurred on every law faculty where I taught as soon as they began to hire female professors with school-age children. If her child became sick at school, the authorities would call the mother and insist she come to take the sick child home or to the hospital. This would have to be done whether it meant missing a class, a committee meeting, or an appointment with a student. The mothers felt guilty. Law school administrators with some reluctance accepted this obligation as overriding. The women naturally were always ready to point out that this was not a dilemma faced by fathers on the faculty.

Then we come to the weakest of conflicts, but still one that creates serious problems. This is the conflict between the client's interests and that of the professional himself. An example is the medical doctor who has an economic interest in a pharmacy or a laboratory and sends all his patients to those businesses from which he receives profits. This type of conflict raises the question of how immediate and large must the economic interest be to influence decisions against the interest of the client? In the complex interdependent world we live in, most of us have at least attenuated financial interests through devices like mutual funds, insurance annuities, or retirement plans in an incredible variety of enterprises with which we must do business. The doctor sending a patient to a pharmacy or laboratory in which he has an ownership interest can with some force make the claim that he is personally acquainted with the quality of the work done in those firms and knows that patients will receive high-quality service.

One context that creates serious ethical problems and belongs either in this section or the next one has developed in contemporary medicine. The vast majority of all medical services today are paid for by a third party, usually a health insurer or a governmental health insurance program. The physician is treating the patient, but is being compensated by an insurer. To whom is the doctor's loyalty owed when making decisions about medical treatment, the patient or the insurer? One can glibly say the patient's wishes and needs must predominate, but if the insurer refuses to pay for the service, the doctor has to furnish it without compensation if the patient cannot afford to pay, furnish it for middle-class patients in many situations where the treatment may bankrupt them, or refuse to treat the patient in fairly clear violation of his Hippocratic oath. If he refuses to treat, is his excuse "I have an overriding duty to the insurer and behind that to the premium payers of the insurer to keep their medical costs down," or is it "I cannot afford to treat you because of financial pressures?" J. L. Austin remarks, "It is worth bearing in mind, too, the general rule that we must not expect to find simple labels for complicated cases."[13]

These examples show that complete avoidance of conflicts of interest is an impossibility. A major role of practical ethics, largely unfulfilled, is to guide people in making priority decisions when there are competing obligations. As long as the formal prohibition is against having conflicts of interest, ethical systems cannot effectively deal with the question of what to do when conflicts exist and cannot be avoided. Every human being is faced with such issues on a daily basis. The more successful the professional, the more serious these conflicts become. More clients will seek her out and expect priority consideration.

The solution currently offered by the code of ethics for lawyers is that a professional may represent clients with potentially conflicting interests if she informs both clients and obtains their consent. That is not a particularly satisfying solution because each client will think he can influence the professional in his favor when resolving such conflicts. Furthermore, the professional has difficult problems in assessing not only the ethics of the choice, but the practicalities, that is, considering alienating which client will be least damaging to her professional practice.

One might deal with such conflicts, as the lawyers have done, by recommending each client be represented by his own lawyer, that is, a competing professional, to protect themselves. That often produces a more adversarial approach to the problem rather than the mediation that many parties hope the professional will provide. In any event, it increases the cost to clients or to the insurance system since hiring two professionals instead of one substantially increases fees (as well as employment opportunities for professionals).

THE IRRESISTIBLE PRESSURE

Another class of excuses is based on the claim that the professional does not have the power to act ethically or that the cost of ethical behavior is too high. This excuse is often used to justify furnishing unnecessary services or padding expenses for clients. It is related to the defenses of duress or necessity, discussed in Chapter 5 on legal defenses, but is used in situations where the legal system would not normally accept the claim as amounting to either duress or necessity. This excuse argues that the element of autonomy or choice was not present. Such freedom exists in all these situations as a matter of theory, but often professionals feel varying degrees of pressure and, at some point, it seems too strong to resist.

In assessing the responsibility of a particular professional under pressure, one can distinguish the following excuses:

(a) "I had to do it to keep up with competitors, either inside or outside the professional working group I belong to." There is a widespread cynical belief that acting ethically places one at a competitive disadvantage. It is difficult to prove or disprove the truth of that belief. A variant of this excuse is the claim that "if I don't do the unethical act and earn the reward, someone else will. If that person is unlikely to suffer penalties, why should he have the reward rather than I?"[14]

This excuse is reinforced by the dominant mode of economic analysis, which emphasizes efficiency and profits as the dominant end of all commercial activity. Ethical conduct is not efficient because time and money costs are entailed that if eliminated would increase the "efficiency" and profitability of the economic enterprise. In a competitive free market unencumbered by governmental regulation, the most successful competitors will be those who do not incur the unnecessary costs of ethical activity. Aspiring competitors must meet that way of doing business.

(b) "I had to do it because my employer told me to or expected me to." In the real world, it is often unnecessary for an employer to *explicitly* order an employee to act in ways that are questionable because of the widely held cynical view that this is expected. Some employers may be consciously or unconsciously using the excuse of transferring responsibility by making the employee the one who can be said to have initiated and then carried out the unethical enterprise. Of course, the employer will reap the rewards of such unethical activity while it is the employee who will receive little reward and take most of the risk.

(c) "Loyalty to the group requires that I participate in unethical activity even if I have reservations." This is a well-recognized ethical dilemma when group loyalty seems to conflict with duties owed to others. It raises the whistle-blower's problem with all its moral difficulties. The power of peer pressure is real and often seems irresistible if one desires to remain a member of the group. In addition to group loyalty, there is a related loyalty to institutions so that professionals may feel compelled by the constraints of their institutional role to do things they would not do as individual and autonomous performers.[15]

(d) "Financial pressures compel unethical behavior." Large organizations of professionals have substantial fixed overhead costs, large investments in technology and in the education of individual professionals, and today even marketing costs.[16] These costs plus adequate compensation for the professionals represent an income floor the organization cannot fall below without going bankrupt. This may not appear to be a serious moral dilemma, because ethical professionals presumably would accept bankruptcy or leave the profession if the only way to continue practice were to pad expenses or provide unnecessary services.[17] A poll of candid professionals would, I suspect, show that not many would agree that bankruptcy was preferable to some degree of overcharging.[18]

Financial pressure can also lead to overwork so that the best level of performance cannot be maintained. A well-known example has been the medical intern or resident who is expected to be on duty for tours of 36 hours or more with little opportunity to rest.[19] Another is the new law firm associate expected to bill 2,200 hours of time to clients a year.[20]

There are three broad ways to deal with these seemingly irresistible pressures that professionals claim push them into unethical activity: either (1) to demand that all professionals be strong enough to resist the pressure, (2) to increase the costs or penalties of unethical activity to the point that the pressure and costs on balance work the other way, or (3) to redesign social structures and the delivery of professional services in ways that minimize such pressures. It is theoretically sounder and less disruptive to select the first alternative and to expect professionals to be strong enough ethically to resist such pressures. That may, however, be so unrealistic that it could force us to take the second or third alternatives more seriously.

One task of practical ethics is to candidly bring these pressures and the dilemmas they force into the open for discussion. Another is to develop some sensible guidelines that work a balance between the degree of pressure that ought to be resisted and the degree of harm caused by unethical action. We would all accept that there are some extreme kinds of harm caused by unethical conduct that the most intense pressure would not justify. On the other hand, severe pressure might be yielded to if little or no harm would result. The proper drawing of lines will never be worked out as long as professional ethics takes a rigid position that it is always unethical to succumb to any such pressures.

THE FAULT OF MACHINES

Another way of disclaiming responsibility is to blame technological failure. Most professional activity today uses complex technology, consisting of machinery and the techniques for using it. Malfunctions can occur in the machinery itself, in communication systems, in techniques, or in integrating the work of various professionals who are masters of specialized technology. One can take the position that the professional is responsible for all technology used in handling a client, but today's technology is so complex that one must often rely on technical experts when the system malfunctions. For example, medical doctors, even though trained in chemistry and pharmacology, rely heavily on drug manufacturers for information about appropriate drugs, side effects, dosages, and so forth. Another example is the occasional need of computer-literate professionals to call upon computer companies, programmers, or repair persons for assistance.

We have been conditioned to think that machines can be made to work perfectly. They are not supposed to possess the human capacity for error. When machines and technology break down, there is the same diffusion of individual responsibility we talked about in considering the excuse of transferring responsibility to another. Was it the designer, the manufacturer, the wholesaler, the installer, the repair person, or the user who committed the human error that led to the machine's malfunction? To this point, both in ethical and legal theory, we are still trying to identify particular individuals who must bear responsibility for technological failure, but that effort begins to seem artificial and unrealistic. No single person can be responsible for the functioning of incredibly complex and integrated technological systems. To select any single one or a small group to bear that responsibility raises the issue of whether it is defensible to ascribe responsibility to a person who has no real control over the situation or the ability to prevent such malfunctioning.

The issue of ability to control or of freedom to act seems to run through all these groups of excuses. The overriding obligation, the irresistible pressure, and the fault of the machines are all situations where the professional did not have or did not feel that he had an option to act in any other way than he did. To the extent that appears to be true, it makes the excuse persuasive. In the modern complex, highly integrated world, we all feel we are increasingly losing control over our lives, so we are not free to act in a sufficient variety of ways to guarantee we have real choice. Lack of such free-dom shrinks the area of true ethical choice and makes ethics seem increasingly irrelevant.

Next, I want to consider two excuses that are often genuine justifications for apparently not complying with ethical obligations, but cannot be described as the result of irresistible pressures that limit choice.

UNFORTUNATE RESULT OF TRIAL AND ERROR

Each profession, along with its individual members, is defined by possession of a particular expertise and that expertise is always being developed and growing. Not only must individual professionals guard and practice that expertise, but also they have to keep current and continue to add to professional knowledge. This often involves trying new and unproved procedures experimentally or on new and unusual problems where there has been little or no experience in the past. The problem with experimentation is that failure or unsuccessful results will often occur. That cannot be avoided while learning by trial and error. Furthermore, much professional activity is judging probabilities, which the ablest professional can occasionally get wrong.

One issue is the nature of each professional's work style. Do we expect professionals to be cautious, careful, and conventional in the performance of their professional expertise? Or do we expect them to be creative, innovative, and experimental? Those represent quite different value choices and character types. A client may have one preference. The professional may have another. There is no inherent necessity that professional or client should be either risk-averse or risk-preferring. We must allow both possibilities under the professional umbrella. One potential difficulty is a mismatch of styles between client and professional. In addition, the client's problem may require one approach rather than the other. Atypical or unusual problems will not respond to conventional practice and one then needs an inventive and risk-preferring professional.

When new and unproven procedures are used and the result is unsuccessful, a client who does not fully understand the nature of professional judgment may complain and the professional must give an explanation or excuse. That excuse will be a claim that he was acting in good faith and trying something new that might have worked, but in this case did not. The best procedure would be to give the explanation before performance. Experimental activity should be agreed to by the client in advance, unless time prevents this in emergency situations. A client who has been informed should be more ready to accept the excuse if the result is less than optimal. We will return to this problem in Chapter 6, but suffice it to say here that it is often an excuse a professional must give and frequently it is justifiable, if not always persuasive. It could, however, also be an alibi to cover the exercise of bad judgment about when experimentation is justified, or else care-lessness in performance.

The scientific or research branch of each profession has in recent decades been more aware of the ethical problems involved in experimental activity. They understand there are constraints on experimentation with human be-ings and that procedures must be followed not unlike the issues of in-formed consent in medicine. Good faith and the careful exercise of judgment are necessary in designing and carrying out experiments where human beings are the subject.

What is not so clearly understood is that the ordinary practice of the pro-fession cannot avoid this problem. In the application of expertise to real and unusual problems that clients bring to professionals, there are these same problems of experimentation, but often there is not sufficient time to care-fully plan and design procedures or solutions. In such contexts, unwished consequences will occur, the client will be unhappy, and it is necessary for the professional to try to explain or excuse himself.

AN ACT OF KINDNESS

Often unethical activity is done out of good motives, particularly a de-sire to be nice or to avoid hurting someone. Does that motive excuse what would otherwise be unethical activity? This often will arise out of conflict-ing obligations where the desire to be nice to one person leads to damaging others.

In correspondence with George Hole, he described for me a problem that is not uncommon for academics, and I assume for all professionals who work with others in a group or bureaucratic setting. He raised a question about a teaching colleague who for the third time secured a sick leave for a dubious psychological reason. He was concerned about the ethics of that colleague and disturbed by the fact that he and other members of his de-partment had to take up the colleague's teaching responsibilities. In re-sponse, I raised a question about his own ethics and that of the fellow teachers who replaced the "ill" professor. Should they have refused to cover for him so that he would have been required to justify his sick leave to the central administration of the university? These authorities would be more likely to balance all the interests and not be influenced by collegial feelings for a fellow department member. What bothered me was I would probably have done the same as George choose to do were I the department chairman, so I replied in a letter that I should add another excuse to my list: "I did it out of kindness." In many cases, this claim may well be more alibi than justification.

Another example where questionable ethics might be justified by this excuse is the practice of many doctors who, when asked by patients to tell them about their medical condition, fudge the truth or lie outright when the situation is one where the patient is suffering from a painful or fatal disease.

This excuse is a clear appeal to motive as grounds of justification. It bears some resemblance to the excuse of overriding obligation since it arises in cases where ethical duties are owed in more than one direction. In the overriding obligation, the issue is whether the selection has been made on the basis of the most important or strongest duty. Here, the issue is whether the motive for selecting one obligation over the other is a decent or a good motive and whether that excuses the damage that is done to other "rightholders."

Now I want to consider three additional excuses, all of which are borrowed more from law than from ethics. These excuses are used from time to time by professionals who have been accused of acting unethically. They do not have anything like the plausibility of the first seven groups of excuses.

THE LACK OF MINIMAL RATIONAL CAPABILITY

Lawyers are used to accepting or at least entertaining a defense that the actor did not have sufficient competence to be legally responsible for his or her acts. In the criminal law, it is the defense of insanity. In commercial transactions, it is the lack of contractual capacity. Should this be an acceptable excuse in ethics, and particularly in professional ethics?

In ethical theory, there is generally an assumption that people will be rational and decent. This is not intended to be descriptive, but rather a starting basis for building the system. Since modern secular ethics is not only a set of principles derived from rational analysis, but an area of voluntary compliance, arguably anyone incapable of understanding ethical guidelines should not be blamed for failure to abide by ethical norms. Would this analysis apply to professional ethics as well?

To achieve the status of a professional through university training, qualifying examinations, and professional licensing, a person must demonstrate much more than the minimal levels of rational competence necessary for legal or ethical responsibility. This set of qualifying conditions would normally make the excuse of lack of capacity unpersuasive when used by professionals.

There is one situation, however, where the claim is often made and might appear plausible. This is where the professional has become addicted to alcohol or drugs. Instead of viewing this as a plausible excuse for unethical conduct, however, it should be grounds for delicensing the professional or at least suspending him from practice until a stage of rehabilitation has been reached where the professional can perform competently and where the excuse would no longer have validity as to future conduct.

THE FAULT OF THE VICTIM

We have recently come to recognize how often one may try to excuse his conduct by saying that it was the fault of the victim. This is particularly common in cases of prejudicial treatment against stereotyped groups or persons. The reason given is that certain characteristics or attitudes of the victims have provoked the action. Can this excuse be used by professionals?

Unethical activity by a professional does not always have an identifiable victim, but usually does. That victim would most commonly be the client, but could be third parties or the public. Among some professionals, there is an attitude of contempt or disparagement for many clients and for most lay people as being unsophisticated, irrational, or incapable of managing their own affairs. This feels much the same as the stereotyped contempt for disfavored racial or ethnic groups.

If we think of the client as victim, how might one try to ground the excuse? It might be that the client lied to the professional. Or it might be that the client did not cooperate. Or perhaps the client was not intelligent enough to understand the advice of the professional or the risks involved, and so on.

This may, at first glance, seem to be a variant, or subcategory, of the excuses labeled "the transfer of responsibility," discussed above. The transfer there was made from one professional to other professionals. There is a qualitative difference when the transfer is made to the victim, particularly when he is a client. The professional-client relationship is one where the professional is ethically committed to protecting the welfare of the client who is purchasing her expertise and skill. This places on the professional the obligation to make sure that the advice is understood, that the professional has the information needed to give that advice, and that the risks associated with the professional activity have been clearly indicated. Responsibility for any damage due to inadequate information or misunderstanding should fall on the professional.

This excuse may be most plausible when the client lies to the professional. All professionals are dependent on having accurate information about the problems of the client. One need think only of the medical history taken by the doctor or the interview by the lawyer to "learn the facts." A professional relying on mistaken or false information will produce a less than optimal result. Most lawyers have learned it is dangerous to rely on clients' stories, even if they are honest and decent people, because their memories may be faulty or they may not understand what is important. How skeptical should professionals be and what is their responsibility to check on clients' stories?

When Clark Clifford, perhaps the savviest and most influential Washington lawyer of his time, was hired by the Bank of Commerce and Credit International (BCCI) to get regulatory permission to operate in the United States and later claimed that BCCI had lied to him just as they had to all their depositors by hiding the fact that they had purchased control of American banks, such as First American Bankshares, that claim rang hollow to the public at large. He, of course, coupled that with the excuse discussed below that merges law and professional ethics arguing that he had done nothing illegal.[21]

WHAT I DID WAS LEGAL

This excuse arises out of accepting a complete correspondence between law and ethics. From this perspective, if the law defines my obligations in terms of right and ethical action and I comply with the law, then what I have done cannot be unethical. As a matter of theory or of logic, this excuse is not plausible, but it is given so often by professionals and other public figures accused of being unethical that it needs to be examined with care.

One could define professional ethics as establishing borders beyond which the professional cannot step without ethical condemnation. This is the result of legalizing professional ethics. As long as professionals stay inside those borders, however close to the line they operate, there are no ethical concerns. This definition accepts ethics as a set of minimal requirements, leaving aspirational ethics out in the cold. Furthermore, even those fairly remote boundary lines may appear insignificant because legal sanctions or effective ethical sanctions are rarely imposed for breaches.

In professional ethics for lawyers, this excuse has taken on more importance with the legalization of professional ethics achieved by reformulating the general guidelines and aspirational principles of the Model Code into the Model Rules containing more precise rules of conduct.[22] The clear rule makes it easier to identify misconduct and to impose punitive consequences for breaches. The persuasiveness of the excuse that I complied with the law and therefore I cannot have been unethical depends very much on how one defines and gives content to professional ethics. The advantages and disadvantages of this approach to ethics will become clearer out of the discussion in the next chapter.

This excuse when used by politicians or professionals who have been accused of unethical conduct and then say the law has not found them guilty of doing anything illegal does not seem to persuade the public they are indeed ethical. There is a strong sense of uneasiness left regarding the character of the actor. Most people feel intuitively that it is a case of category confusion. Moving from "not illegal" to "being ethical" is a double confusion. The same connotation to "not illegal" in ethics is not "ethical" but rather "not unethical." "Not illegal" does not necessarily imply "clearly legal," and "clearly legal" does not imply "clearly ethical."

The confusion between law and ethics is understandable and difficult to avoid. When we are in an area of overlap where the conduct is governed both by law and by ethics, the major concern of the actor will be with the law because of its more social and public aspects and because of the greater severity of the sanctions. Even if one is concerned primarily with the legal category and consequences, this inevitably also raises ethical concerns. This is why so many professionals being sued for malpractice regard the finding of a jury that they have acted improperly as carrying ethical condemnation, even if the suit is not intended to criticize the professional, but merely to unlock his insurance protection to pay compensation to the victim.

The ideology known as neoconservatism argues strongly for deregulation and a minimalist government. Coupled with this excuse, that position comes close to creating ethical anarchy; that is, there are almost no constraints on self-interested human activity. If these two factors are joined with the argument that the invisible hand of the market or the self-interest of sophisticated consumers will be sufficient to protect against unethical activity, there is for many professionals, at least on the conscious level, the removal of serious ethical constraints.

I want to conclude this chapter with an incident from my early professional life that consciously raised for me for the first time the issue of ethical excuses made by professionals, in this case, myself. During my first year in practice in Oklahoma, I was handed a small case by the legal partner I worked for. Our client managed for his mother a piece of rural property on which there were oil wells. He had hired a pumper, whose job was to oversee the pumping equipment. The pumper sued our client under the Federal Fair Labor Standards Act for overtime pay and penalties, claiming he had worked more than forty hours a week through the entire period of employment. We felt there was little merit to the claim because there was not close to forty hours of work to be done. Many pumpers spent much of their daytime hours hunting and fishing, and we suspected that was the case here. Since it was an isolated property, it would have been difficult to prove that fact.

The federal law had a tight statute of limitations that expired week by week and barred all claims not filed within one year of the employment period for which the pay was sought. The claimant had sued the wrong person, since the owner of the property was the one who hired him.[23] Our client was merely her agent. It seemed to me as a neophyte lawyer a sensible strategy to wait and let the period of the statute elapse and then notify the claimant's attorney he had sued the wrong person. In the normal course, that would have worked but the judge decided to clear his docket up and so the case was set for trial three weeks before the statute would have run on the entire claim.

I was told to negotiate with the lawyer for the claimant. When I explained the situation, I was astonished that he thought my course of action unethical. If he had sued the wrong person because of lack of knowledge of the true status of the parties, he felt I had an ethical duty to inform him so he could sue the right party and have the case decided on the merits. Since I regarded myself as ethical, I was highly offended by his accusation. On consulting a number of other attorneys in the area, about half thought I had acted unethically and the other half found nothing wrong with what I had done.

Now to the problem of excuses. I was genuinely unaware that there was an ethical issue. Is that an acceptable excuse? My legal education, which did include a course in the legal profession and ethics, had not prepared me to deal with such a problem. Was that a violation of the duty of my teachers and, if so, was their failure to perform their responsibilities, an acceptable excuse for my conduct? Did I in fact have an ethical duty to inform the attorney on the other side that he had sued the wrong party? The resolution of that depends on how much I follow the informal code of conduct about duties between fellow professionals and how much I adhere to ultimate loyalty to the client's interests. Is that conflict of duties an acceptable excuse for choosing either alternative? Does a good motive, the difficulty of proving on the merits that the claim was weak, justify using the technical defense to reach, what in my judgment, was the right result? Is that an acceptable excuse? Forty years later, I still find these issues difficult.

NOTES

1. The caveat as to doctors arises out of a relatively new problem, the obligation of doctors to report cases of suspected child abuse, even when it is the parent who brings the child to the doctor, tells her about the injury, and is the paying client. In addition, some medical associations are seriously considering amending their formal ethical rule on confidentiality to require doctors to notify police if a patient makes a threat about killing someone else. See Jane Gadd, "MD Reporting of Threats Wins Backing," THE GLOBE AND MAIL, Toronto (Tuesday, July 11, 1996): A3.

2. For a nice account, with examples, of medical doctors being unaware of the presence of moral issues see Samuel Gorovitz, DOCTORS' DILEMMAS: MORAL CONFLICT AND MEDICAL CARE (New York: Macmillan, 1982), pp. 15–21.

3. See my discussion of the teacher's responsibility in McDowell, "The Ethical Obligations of Professional Teachers (of Ethics)," PROFESSIONAL ETHICS: A MULTIDISCIPLINARY JOURNAL, Vol. 1, Nos. 3 & 4 (1992): 53.

4. Christopher Lasch, THE CULTURE OF NARCISSISM: AMERICAN LIFE IN AN AGE OF DIMINISHING EXPECTATIONS (New York: Warner Books, 1979), p. 209.

5. If, however, the professional charged with acting unethically tries to pass it on to subordinates over whom he has control, such as younger professional associates or staff, the excuse is not very effective. He must accept responsibility for their weaknesses since he selected, ought to have monitored, and could have discharged them.

6. The character appears in Ross Thomas's popular set of novels, CHINAMAN'S CHANCE, OUT ON THE RIM, and VOODOO, LTD.

7. An interesting variant, which is now evolving, is the merger of two separate groups of professionals into an integrated business organization. There has been a movement of multinational management and consulting firms to acquire ownership of law firms as a part of the service they offer their clients. See Kevin Marron, "Lawyers Wary as Mjultinationals Eye Their Turf," THE GLOBE AND MAIL, Toronto (August 12, 1997): B27.

8. One well-known example of this problem was the Hyatt Regency disaster in Kansas City, Missouri, where on July 7, 1981, a skywalk in the lobby collapsed, killing 114 people and seriously injuring scores of others. There were ongoing disputes about whether the collapse was the fault of the owners, the architects, the design engineers, the general contractor, subcontractors, or suppliers. The liability to injured parties ran into the tens of millions of dollars. See *Firestone v. Crown Center Redevelopment Corporation*, 693 S.W.2d (Mo. en banc, 1985).

9. Thomas Nagel, "Ruthlessness in Public Life," in PUBLIC AND PRIVATE MORALITY, Stuart Hampshire, ed. (Cambridge: Cambridge University Press, 1978), p. 76.

10. Perhaps the best example is the liability imposed on manufacturers for injuries caused to consumers by defective products. An influential statement of the theory is found in the American Law Institute, Restatement of the Law of Torts, Second, § 402A: Special Liability of Seller of Product for Physical Harm to User or Consumer.

(1) One who sells any product in a defective condition unreasonably dangerous to the user or consumer or to his property is subject to liability for physical harm thereby caused to the ultimate user or consumer, or to his property if

(a) the seller is engaged in the business of selling such a product, and

(b) it is expected to and does reach the user or consumer without substantial change in the condition in which it is sold.

(2) The rule stated in Subsection (1) applies although

(a) the seller has exercised all possible care in the preparation and sale of his product, and

(b) the user or consumer has not bought the product from or entered into any contractual relation with the seller.

11. This same sort of questionable assumption about group behavior seems to underlie a proposal by some advisors to the Clinton health care task force who in 1993 advocated prohibiting malpractice suits against doctors and imposing liability only on insurance companies and health maintenance organizations, so-called enterprise liability. They justified this on the grounds that such corporate entities would monitor performance by individual practitioners. See Robert Pear, "Clinton Advisers Outline a Big Shift for Malpractice," NEW YORK TIMES (Friday, May 21, 1993) A1, col. 6.

12. Nagel, "Ruthlessness in Public Life," p. 81.

13. J. L. Austin, "A Plea for Excuses," PHILOSOPHICAL PAPERS, 3d ed. (Oxford: Oxford University Press, 1979), p. 195.

14. The childhood variant of this excuse is "My friend did the same thing and was not punished by his parents, so it is unfair for you to punish me."

15. See quote from Thomas Nagel, *supra* n. 7.

16. Until recently, it was a violation of ethics for many professions to advertise or solicit clients. The total ban on advertising was invalidated by the U.S. Supreme Court as violating the First Amendment in *Bates v. State Bar of Arizona*, 433 U.S. 350 (1977). The ban on soliciting was invalidated in *Shapero v. Kentucky Bar Assn.*, 486 U.S. 466 (1988). This has created substantial financial pressure on professionals to spend money in merchandising activity to meet competition.

17. This problem of overcharging and what the professions might do about it was a central subject of Banks McDowell, ETHICAL CONDUCT AND THE PROFESSIONAL'S DILEMMA: CHOOSING BETWEEN SERVICE AND SUCCESS (Westport, Conn.: Quorum Books), 1991.

18. One can argue that the true cost to a client requires allocating the fixed overhead and other costs of practice. Thus spreading this cost among clients is not unethical. When the number of clients fall below an acceptable number to bear the costs at a reasonable figure, the ethical dilemma of leaving the profession or overcharging is present, however. Competitive pressures could in theory prevent overcharging, but this requires sophisticated customers who shop among professionals and who can make sound decisions about the value of services, conditions that are seldom present when a client hires a professional.

19. See Joseph Berger, "The Long Days and Short Life of a Medical Student; Relatives Say Fatigue May Have Had a Role in the Car Crash that Killed Frank Ingulli," NEW YORK TIMES (Sunday, May 30, 1993): sec. 1, p. 39, col. 2.

20. See Elizabeth M. Fowler, "Reducing the Stress on Lawyers," NEW YORK TIMES (January 23, 1990): C17. 2,200 hours, which works out to 40 hours per week, may not seem like an unreasonable request, but one cannot ethically identify a particular client to bill for many activities. Furthermore, a new associate may well not have enough business to make up 40 hours per week. The pressure to overcharge some clients by claiming more time than actually spent and also to attribute general or indirect activities to a client chosen at random may be irresistible.

21. The New York criminal prosecution was ultimately dismissed by prosecutors, partly because of Mr. Clifford's poor health. See Richard Perez-Pena, "New York to Drop Clifford Charges," NEW YORK TIMES (Tuesday, November 2, 1993): B7.

22. The Model Code of Professional Responsibility was adopted by the American Bar Association in 1908 and contains nine canons of a very high level of ethical generality, supplemented by Disciplinary Rules and Ethical Considerations. The Model Rules of Professional Conduct were adopted by the American Bar Association in 1983 and consists of 55 detailed rules followed by Comments. See Thomas D. Morgan and Ronald D. Rotunda, eds., MODEL CODE OF PROFESSIONAL RESPONSIBILITY, MODEL RULES OF PROFESSIONAL CONDUCT AND OTHER SELECTED STANDARDS (Mineola, N.Y.: Foundation Press, 1996).

23. This was before discovery procedures became widely used, so the attorney for the other side was not negligent in failing to discover the truth.

4

Law and Ethics:
The Different Systems

Throughout this book, I will be drawing comparisons between the legal system and systems of ethics, so it is important to understand the ways they are similar and the important differences between them. The two systems are often confused, the most common and dangerous confusion producing the excuse that as long as I follow the law, I cannot be accused of being unethical.

Law and ethics are both normative systems prescribing guidelines on how people ought to live their lives. And because people are not always legal or ethical in their behavior, both systems face the problem of excuses or defenses offered when a person is charged with having violated a standard of behavior.

The two systems have a great degree of overlap. Many of our controlling norms are both legal and ethical. While law and ethics are in general mutually supportive, the overlap is far from complete, so the systems can conflict. This raises the oldest of all problems for political and legal theory—how one should resolve such a conflict between law and morality. When there is such a conflict, one might believe the legal rule unjust and choose to disobey it. Conversely, one could conclude that even if the law calls for conduct violating the actor's personal ethics, he still has to comply because of the overriding importance of fidelity to the law. The argument supporting this latter position is that if social and political stability is desirable, everybody needs to obey a valid law whether he agrees with it or not.[1]

Serious conflicts between law and ethics are not common in ordinary life, and that set of issues is not particularly relevant to the problem of excuses, except when the excuse given is that one normative system requires that the other be disobeyed. Occasionally, an argument is made in court that illegal conduct is excused on moral grounds.[2] More often, someone accused of acting unethically makes the claim that nothing illegal was done, implicitly arguing that it was therefore not unethical. This contention was listed in the last chapter as one of the ethical excuses.

One clarification about how I use the terms "legal system" and "lawyer," on the one hand, and "ethics" or "ethicist," on the other. "Lawyer" is not restricted to people trained and licensed as professional lawyers. We all know of the "jailhouse lawyer" and of people more legalistic than most lawyers. Nor does "ethicist" mean only a professional philosopher. I refer to two different styles of thought or culture about how social dysfunction should be dealt with. One approach, increasingly widespread and popular, is to enact clear and specific rules of conduct and have those enforced by legal processes and sanctions. That approach of regulating human conduct is what I mean by law or lawyers. The best lawyers are not limited to that attitude. Ethicists are more concerned with principles and general guidelines about conduct, emphasize the importance of character, and are more skeptical about the efficacy of rigid social enforcement. There are trained lawyers who could be described as such ethicists.

The fact that the two systems of law and equity are often confused has operated to the detriment of viewing issues as ethical ones. An example is the case of former Senator Packwood of Oregon. Female secretaries and associates accused him of sexual harassment over a long period of time. In addition, he was accused of trying to influence a lobbyist to give his former wife a job, and of altering his diaries after a subpoena from the Senate Ethics Committee. Due to the Senate Ethics Committee's recommendation of expulsion, Senator Packwood resigned.[3]

News commentators regularly referred to his problems as ethical ones and there is no question that he acted unethically in abusing his position of power over subordinate female employees, and in using his political position to gather favors for his former wife. Are we not, however, talking about legal problems? He was investigated by the Justice Department and by the Senate Ethics Committee. All three sets of alleged offenses were to some degree illegal. Certainly the Attorney General has no authority to investigate and prosecute people for anything other than illegal activities. From what can be gathered from the newspapers, the approach of the Senate Ethics Committee was much the same. Did he violate the clear rules and, if so, what sort of sanction should the Senate impose?

The public description of these activities that were clearly illegal but characterized as issues of ethics raises a series of questions. Are professional ethics really no longer matters of ethics, but of legal rules? Should we recognize and accept that professional ethics as a term has been co-opted by the legal rules of professional practice? Is there anything wrong with that?

Is there still an area outside the legal rules of professional practice that is or should be governed by more traditional notions of ethics? Is that area the zone of professional autonomy where the actions of professionals are primarily matters of judgment?

In this chapter, I want to address three questions. The first is the different characteristics of law and ethics. What are their differing roles and what are the structures and ideas necessary to deal with those roles? Second, how do these differences affect the way excuses in ethics and defenses in law are used? Third, what is the proper role for law and the appropriate sphere of ethics in governing professional conduct? In other words, should we think of professional responsibility as belonging more to the sphere of law or of ethics?

THE DIFFERING CHARACTERISTICS OF LAW AND ETHICS

J. L. Austin said law was one of the sources one could look to in trying to understand the way excuses work in language and in ethics. Since I look at these problems from the law side of the divide, that is an approach I sympathize with. But Stuart Hampshire has cautioned us that

> the analogy with law, which is usually invoked to illuminate reasoning about moral questions, also cannot be pressed too far in the opposite direction. The thought that enters into a legal decision must always be reconstructible as a potential argument in further justification of that decision. There must also be a known record of earlier relevant cases and decisions, and not a confused memory of an indefinite multiplicity of parallel cases.[4]

Lawyers are trained to think differently from the way philosophers are trained to reason. The difference is not just that between theoretical or applied approaches to problem solving. Legal reasoning is highly formalized, is carefully limited to the particular problem at hand, relies on careful records of similar cases, and is constrained by the necessity to reach a socially acceptable result.[5] Since lawyers and ethicists are often concerned with the same problems, why the differences in approach? To help understand the answer to that question, I want to discuss five practical issues: the scope of coverage of the two systems, the clarity and formulation of duties in each, how breach is established in each, the consequences of breach, and the relationship between the two systems.

Scope of Coverage

Lawyers and political scientists are always interested in questions of jurisdiction. Where does a governing system reach and what are the borders beyond which it has no authority? Ethics and law are both governing schemes. The area of life covered by ethics is broader than that regulated by law. One can seriously contend that all aspects of life are governed by ethics. Whether one thinks of rule theorists, like Bernard Gert, or virtue theorists, like Alisdair MacIntyre, ethical systems and their precepts seem designed to reach all people and most, if not all, of their conduct.

Law is more modest in reach. Sizable areas of human activity are intentionally left unregulated. There is a strong commitment in Anglo-American law to leaving unconstrained a broad area of free choice. In addition, there are other contexts where for a variety of public policies and prudential concerns, the law does not occupy territory clearly covered by ethics. Here are two examples well known to all first-year law students.

The first is a common hypothetical posed in torts classes. If a person, while walking along the bank of a lake, notices someone in danger of drowning and shouting for help, does she have a legal duty to try to save him? The answer is no, although most people would say she has an ethical duty to try to rescue him.[6] Furthermore, many people would act on that duty. The law does not reach this case for practical or administrative reasons. There may be many explanations why one refrains from saving the drowning person. She may not actually have heard the shouts. She may have been physically frail and unable to help. She may have been hurrying on an emergency mission, such as visiting her sick child in the hospital. And, of course, she may be totally indifferent to the fate of the drowning person, or actually take enjoyment from watching the death struggle. To open up such an area for legal remedies would lead to difficulty in defining standards followed by messy litigation about her motives, knowledge, other options, and so on. Moreover, the ethical injunction usually works well enough to guarantee assistance.

The second is the well-known old Massachusetts contracts case of *Mills v. Wyman*.[7] The defendant was the father of an adult sailor. On returning from a voyage, the seaman was taken seriously ill in Connecticut and was nursed by the plaintiff as an act of charity. The sailor died. After his son's death, the father learned of plaintiff's kindness and wrote a letter promising to pay all his expenses. The father later reneged on this promise. The good samaritan sued on the promise. When the case was appealed, a legendary Chief Justice of Massachusetts denied recovery on the grounds that the promise lacked consideration. Chief Justice Parker made clear in the opinion that he had total contempt for the father who made the promise and then refused to perform, saying:

> General rules of law established for the protection and security of honest and fair minded men, who may inconsiderately make promises without any equivalent, will sometimes screen men of a different character from engagements which they are bound in *foro conscientiae*

to perform. . . . The rule that a mere verbal promise, without any consideration, cannot be enforced by action is universal in its application,
and cannot be departed from to suit particular cases in which a refusal
to perform such a promise may be disgraceful.

The father's duty was only ethical. The legal doctrine of consideration limits enforceable promises to those that are serious and for which a valuable
exchange was given. The judge felt it would warp the law of contract to
turn the father's undertaking into an enforceable promise. Interestingly
enough, this and similar cases are discussed in the law of contracts under
the rubric "moral obligation."

The issue of the jurisdiction of the two systems is central in dealing with
the excuse that complying with the law is the only ethical requirement for
professionals. H.L.A. Hart summarized an argument of Jeremy Bentham as
to why it was necessary to keep the two systems carefully separated as a
matter of clear thinking.

> Bentham found that the confusion [between law and morals] had
> spread symmetrically in two different directions. On the one hand
> Bentham had in mind the anarchist who argues thus: "This ought not
> to be the law, therefore it is not and I am free not merely to censure but
> to disregard it." On the other hand he thought of the reactionary who
> argues: "This is the law, therefore it is what it ought to be," and thus
> stifles criticism at its birth.[8]

Clear thinking and analysis as well as right living requires that one understand and use each system in its proper sphere. We are not much concerned
with what Hart called the "anarchist's" contention, but professionals and
other public figures have used the reactionary's argument as an excuse
when charged with unethical activity. Professional ethics is often an area of
confusion about whether we are talking law or ethics.

The Formality and Precision of the Duty

We commonly describe legal standards as rules. In ethics, we talk about
principles or standards. This linguistic distinction captures the difference
in the degree of specificity and precision about the guidelines in the two
systems.[9]

Legal duties are formal, public, socially agreed on, and determinable. If
there is doubt, one major role of lawyers is to inform clients what their duties are. Legal duties are created in a variety of ways. In a democracy, many
rules are enacted by elected legislators. In theory, the rules are debated and
chosen by representatives who know what the social consensus is or is
likely to be. The executive bureaucracy formulates specialized and detailed

regulations. In common-law jurisdictions, a high percentage of our formal legal rules are still created by judges as a product of resolving disputes, the process of *stare decisis*. These common-law rules are more likely to be tied by analogy to past practices than current sentiments, but judges are far from indifferent to contemporary values.

In prescribing duties, law is more limited and precise than ethics. Law, for example, in defining its prohibition against taking life, creates important exceptions, self-defense and justifiable homicide, and within the crime of homicide creates lesser degrees of wrongdoing, manslaughter or negligent homicide, which carry lighter penalties. Ethical theorists might claim to work with the same distinctions, but they probably ought not to take that position. Their project is different, to create a view toward the value of life, particularly human life, and instill a strong feeling against destroying or damaging it.[10]

When we talk about ethics, it is not nearly as clear or determinable what our ethical duties are. The social consensus about ethics exists only at a rather abstract level. Most of us accept that it is not open to argue as a justification for breach that I live under a different legal system than my fellow citizens. I can, however, contend that my moral system differs at significant points from that of my fellow citizens and I have done so on a good number of occasions, invariably to the disadvantage of the moral systems of others. When it comes to deciding on context-specific rules that should control ethical choices, the disagreements about duty widen even more.

Legal norms generally represent a minimum social code of conduct everybody can be expected to comply with. The judge and jury should apply the same rule and standards to the defendant's conduct no matter what his particular abilities or competencies are. The law attains some individualizing by creating subclasses. For example, a professional's duty to perform his duties competently gets tested through a malpractice action. The standard is a professional must perform his duties as competently as the average professional in his specialty and area of practice. Inside the general class of people, we create a subclass of professionals, and a further subclass of specialists, but the same standards apply to every member of each class.

The degree of competence in the performance of services required by ethics is quite different. I have argued elsewhere that a professional's ethical duty is to perform at the highest levels of competence she can achieve, or to use a currently popular expression, to strive for excellence.[11] If her abilities, training, and competencies are above average, she cannot ethically perform at average levels. Nor can she argue that her performance is still what the majority of professionals would do and thus meets her ethical duty. Ethics, a system of voluntary compliance without the compulsory sanctions of law, can and should be more personalized and demanding.

The difference in the universality between legal and ethical is not absolute, but a matter of degree. Contract law permits highly individualized legal rules. Because we believe in a free and individualistic society, contract empowers parties to create legal rules, which are a matter of personal choice and fit their particular needs and wishes.

The Process of Establishing Breach

Since courts are primarily interested in affixing responsibility on identified persons in order to attach legal consequences, the questions of whether there was a breach and who committed it are as important as establishing the duty. There is a clearly defined procedure about how one establishes breach. While a court's decision may not always be right, the procedure is designed to resolve disputed matters as honestly as fair-minded human beings can. Ethicists are less concerned with the practical problems inherent in locating the presence of this element.

One fundamental difference is the set of presumptions about whether a person is responsible. There is little doubt about the appropriateness of imposing ethical duties on people in general or on professionals. In contrast, law has always been reluctant to impose liability. In criminal law, one starts from a presumption of innocence. A person accused of a crime need not offer a defense at all. The prosecution must offer enough evidence to convict the defendant beyond a reasonable doubt. Only at that point is it logically or practically necessary to offer defenses. And, of course, if any defense offered is persuasive, the defendant is entitled to be acquitted.

In its starting assumptions, the civil law differs from criminal law only in matters of degree. The attitude of early tort and contract law was that losses should lie where they fell unless the plaintiff could prove there was a valid reason for transferring the loss to another. In tort law, it was necessary to establish that the defendant's wrongful act caused the injury to plaintiff or his property. Only when that was established by a preponderance of the evidence was it necessary for the defendant to offer defenses. In commercial transactions, the injured party must prove that the defendant had contracted to assume the loss or to accomplish a result that did not happen. If the plaintiff could not prove a contract existed, the defendant was entitled to judgment without offering defenses.

The law is not only a normative system, but also equally a mechanism for dispute resolution. In fact, common-law lawyers tend to define law more as a way of resolving disputes than as a normative system. A complex system of social structures and procedures has evolved to be invoked when people cannot resolve their disputes by compromise or consensus. At trial, each party is represented by a lawyer who presents to the court every argument in favor of her client's case. This includes not only presenting the facts in a favorable light, but also making all the arguments on the law and justice of the competing claims. In this process of deciding whether a defendant has breached a duty to the plaintiff, all of defendant's excuses or defenses will be considered, evaluated, and either rejected or given weight.

From these experiences of refining defenses, which have been going on for centuries, ethics may learn from the law.

The Consequences of Being Responsible

When one is found responsible for some illegal act, a wide range of sanctions is available. Those legal penalties clearly pertaining to professional activity are criminal prosecutions for grossly negligent or intentional injuries to clients, fraud or conversion actions for misappropriation of client's property, malpractice actions for negligent injuries, and delicensing for professionals found incompetent or unethical.

The sanctions for acting unethically are less definite. These include blame, loss of reputation, and guilt. Any of these can be effective and severe penalties, but such ethical sanctions are less clearly present nor can they be apportioned to the degree of unethical activity as are legal penalties for illegal acts. There is the irony that those people least to blame because they are the most ethical in disposition are likely to feel such penalties more strongly than would amoral or immoral people.

The matter of reputation is important for professionals even in these times of the breakdown of small communities and long-term relationships between professionals and clients. When looking for professional services, sophisticated clients will not select at random, but will inquire of former clients or others who know about the individual professional or the professional group. The potential client's questions will not only be about the professional's technical competence, but also about his ethical character. Is this a person I can trust and who will be fair with me? Neither advertising nor manipulation of prospective clients can overcome a negative reputation. The professional may not even learn of a bad report that cost him clients, so it is important to protect his professional reputation both as to competence and as to trustworthiness. This may explain why many medical doctors react so strongly to a claim of malpractice, which goes not only to questions of technical competence, but to questions of trust. If the client had sufficient confidence in the professional, he might have accepted the professional's explanation of why the injury occurred.

This significant difference in the social and personal consequences between being held legally responsible and being ethically responsible explains the degree of importance people attach to each system. One does makes choices by anticipating the consequences of various options. In our modern cynical and secular society, legal penalties are of greater concern than are ethical consequences. Because of this, pure ethical obligations can recede in importance.

The Relationship between the Two Systems

While law and ethics have different purposes and zones of operation, they overlap in many of their normative standards and functions. The interaction between them is complex. Enacting legal norms based on ethical standards authenticates those ethical principles politically and socially. Legal proceedings can then be used to compel compliance. There are specified procedures by which a society enacts a legal norm and when that is done, one can say with confidence the rule has been approved and accepted by society. There is no such formal procedure to authenticate ethical norms.

Statutory adoption of ethical norms followed by lax enforcement may be a signal that appearance, rather than compliance, is what matters. Repealing a legal norm so it reverts to an unenforceable ethical one may indicate that the society as a political entity does not regard the standard as important or at least as universally acceptable. There may be other reasons, of course, for delegalizing a standard, such as the wish to encourage freedom of choice, change in value positions in the society, or administrative difficulties in legal enforcement.

If compliance with standards is our primary concern, moving from ethical injunction to legal command as a way of compelling obedience may not be satisfactory. Legal processes have not been particularly successful in forcing compliance in a world corrupted by dysfunctional systems and bad organization. We have not minimized violent crime in inner-city neighborhoods where unemployment is high, educational systems crumbling, and capital investment almost non-existent. Moving to social arenas more directly involving professionals, we have not eliminated or much minimized business fraud, political corruption, banker mismanagement, Medicare fraud, insurance fraud, or lawyers pursuing frivolous suits. This may partly explain why lawyers prefer to see themselves as resolvers of disputes rather than as regulators of human activity.

Why do people act in the ways that are socially desirable? What part does ethics play and what influence does law have? People, while acting, are seldom conscious of what the law requires except in the most general way. Their ethical (or value) system, learned from childhood about the right thing to do in various contexts, is more likely to control conduct. Oliver Wendell Holmes, Jr. saw a century ago that the major function of law was to deal with those people whose moral or ethical systems are out of kilter with those of normal people.[12] The compulsory machinery of law generally deals with people whose moral compass is not reliable or else resolves disputes even decent people are unable to settle by normal mechanisms of consensus or compromise.

The proper sphere of law and ethics is not so much a theoretical one based on the analysis of their roles, but depends on how the line is drawn in a particular time and context. One striking feature of our modern complex society, where communities and common shared values have broken down, is the increased way we resort to law to resolve matters that earlier would have been handled in less contentious, expensive, and socially destructive ways. There may well be some negative correlation between the ethical and social health of the society and the degree to which resort is made to the compulsory, authoritative, and costly procedures afforded by the law.

Ethical concepts have always had influence on the creation and application of law. Lawmaking activity is not only the formal creation of rules, that is, legislating. It is also the working out of the rules in the common-law process of formulating holdings out of cases and deciding when and how to apply various legal principles. Lawyers have always understood that ethical ideas are influential in these less formal processes of lawmaking and application.

While one can say that ethics influences law, is the converse true? Does or should law influence ethics? Can ethicists learn from the process of formulating legal defenses and the particular defenses that have been developed out of resolving legal controversies?[13] That is one of the important questions this book addresses.

THE DIFFERENCES BETWEEN THE WAY LEGAL DEFENSES AND EQUITABLE EXCUSES WORK

As a result of the law serving as the ultimate mechanism for resolving disputes, certain features have evolved in contrast with ethics. One is a special class of experts, the lawyers, whose role is not only to advise disputants about legal rights and duties, but also to mediate between them and the social institutions designed to resolve their problems. These are primarily the courts, but include the police, administrative agencies, and, on occasion, legislatures. In contrast, there is no class of ethical specialists we turn to when in doubt about the ethical thing to do. There was a time when priests, ministers, and rabbis fulfilled that role, but in a society that has become increasingly secular, they are seldom consulted now in that particular way.

Defense lawyers, charged with trying to avoid having their clients found responsible, are committed to developing and working with defenses. The defenses used by lawyers are more formal and may bear only limited relation to the excuses that the defendant himself gave for the behavior in question. In many disputes, one party will have offered an excuse to the other for his untoward behavior and that excuse was rejected. That does not mean a lawyer cannot come up with a defense that will be successful at the trial.

The consequences of being responsible are different for the two systems. Ethics is largely a system of voluntary compliance relying on internal sanctions such as guilt or on less compulsory sanctions like the loss of respect or contempt from fellow citizens. An actor who is indifferent to such consequences can ignore ethical obligations. In contrast, the parties have little choice but to accept a legal resolution of their dispute. Compulsory remedies backed by the authority and power of the state compel acceptance of the court's decision and obedience to it, except in the most extreme cases of conscientious objection.

The professionalism of lawyers and the severity of consequences has placed a different focus on how one establishes duty and breach. In cases of doubt, there is a presumption against legal liability. No such presumption is at work in ethics. The charge of having acted unethically is usually made by victims or others who have not been trained or given good guidelines about the dangers of making such allegations or the difficulties of proving the elements of unethical action. Nor are ethical excuses given by actors who have been formally trained about the nature and importance of excuses. A frequent complaint of children, as well as adults, is that the parent or other person who makes a claim of unethical activity did not give them a chance to explain or prove they were not responsible.

Litigation in court will ultimately produce a clear black-and-white decision, either guilty or not, legally responsible or not. In order to reach a clear decision, complex fact situations and subtle distinctions and arguments are often reduced to simple questions with clear answers. The one option not available to a court is to refuse to decide.[14] We know whether a legal defense works or not. We are less sure about ethical excuses.

The greater severity of legal consequences seems to make it easier to say someone is ethically responsible than that he is legally responsible. While it may be easier in law than in ethics to decide what the duty is and whether there has been a breach, it is more difficult to decide whether to impose the consequences for legal responsibility. That is why legal defenses are often more successful than excuses in avoiding or mitigating responsibility.

THE RESPECTIVE SPHERES OF LAW AND ETHICS IN PROFESSIONAL ETHICS

Ethics, designed to tell people how they ought to act, focuses on the actor and contains guidelines to help him make the myriad of moral choices an individual faces. Law is designed to constrain those actions by which other people are adversely affected and that upset social peace. The legal focus is more on the victim. A major purpose, particularly of civil law, is to achieve corrective justice by transfer payments from actor to victim to restore imbalances caused by illegal acts.[15] The justification for such interference must be strong and legal intervention ought to be limited to serious cases of injustice. This makes the role of defenses in the law more critical in achieving proper balances than that of excuses in ethics.

In professional activity, the law is essential to ensure that professionals meet minimum obligations of professional practice and that their clients and other victims are compensated for unethical activity that has caused damage. This is the purpose of malpractice actions as well as actions to delicense professionals who consistently fall below acceptable minimum standards.

When the two systems overlap, there is the strongest social compulsion and cohesion. Ethical people will voluntarily comply with the joint rules because of the ethical obligation. Amoral people will comply with the joint rules only to the extent they fear legal penalties. Choices that amoral people make will be constrained by the legal, but not the ethical, system.

There are two problems with leaving this joint area of coverage exclusively to the law. The first is efficacy. Unless a substantial majority of people comply with the rules because they view them as ethically obligatory, the society will become either an anarchy or else a police state, which succeeds in controlling conduct only as long as fear of punishment is real.

The incipient tendencies of all people, particularly professionals, to be ethical should be fostered. What we are discussing here is the problem of motive, what was referred to earlier as an "explanation" for action. Motives are always complex and mixed, but there are at least three important ones controlling choices made by professionals. One is to make money. Another is to avoid legal sanctions. A third is to do the right or ethical thing. A major goal for law and ethics is to constrain the unbridled drive to make money at all costs. This is not an easy task. The dominance of an extreme free-market ideology emphasizing the profit motive, an extreme competitiveness to be the most successful as measured by income, the breakdown of community and relational constraints, and the loss of spiritual or religious values have all merged to leave many professionals with a predominant goal, to achieve maximum financial success.[16] Professional ethics courses can emphasize that constraints on this drive are rule and sanction oriented, which is the lawyer's approach. Or professional ethics courses could stress that those constraints are ones of ethics, moral character, and decency.

The second reason for emphasizing the ethical over the legal is territorial. If one wants as a matter of political theory or personal values to have a wide area of autonomy, it is necessary to keep such an area unconstrained, which can occur only by leaving it to the exclusive realm of the ethical.

It is in the sphere where law chooses not to control that ethics becomes of essential importance. As Andre Brink has written: "Wherever, and in whatever context, freedom is tested and defined, the weight of moral choice is involved."[17] When professionals acting in the arena of professional autonomy are tempted to conduct themselves with less than appropriate propriety or else might fail to exercise sound judgment, they need ethical and aspirational guidelines. If the only purpose of professional ethics is to ensure minimally acceptable professional behavior, we hardly need talk of professional *ethics*. The law is sufficient to deal with those kinds of transgressions.

In acting as an autonomous professional, there are difficult choices to be made. The ethical problems that worry decent professionals are interwoven with the exercise of good technical judgment in specific contexts.

The ethical dimension must be part of the repertoire of exercising good professional judgment taught by teachers and mentors whenever professional judgment is being exercised.[18] Ethical behavior is learned and professional ethical behavior must be learned in and after professional school. The form of the ethical norm cannot be primarily black-and-white rules, but principles, guidelines, priority processes in choosing between options, and so on. Although it may sound old-fashioned, it is here that one must be concerned with character issues and virtues, rather than rules.

Thus, my conceptual definition of professional ethics is both territorial and functional. Territorial in the sense that it covers the area left unregulated by the law of professional practice. Functional in the sense that it gives working guidelines on how one must operate in that area of professional autonomy if one wants to be labeled a professional of good moral character.

Whether professional ethics ought to be thought of as ethics or of law is not merely a matter of accurate description. There are important values or policies that should control the choice of category. The professions have always jealously guarded the personal autonomy of the individual practitioner. Much activity of individual professionals should be outside the realm of legal or governmental or even professional regulation. This is defensible because much professional work involves complex and context-specific judgments about wiser courses of action on behalf of a particular client. Often the client and professional know each other well and many professionals are chosen by sophisticated clients for their nonconventional and above-average skills. The best of these professionals want to be free from having to justify their decisions even to other professionals who may be more conventional or less able than they are.

Unfortunately, freedom can be abused and clients or the public seriously injured by greedy, incompetent, or unscrupulous professionals. We are willing to trust freedom to ethical and decent human beings who will make defensible judgments. We are more likely to regulate activity if we suspect it will lead to unjust results. Thus, the legal or governmental decision to give wide autonomy to professionals is linked to the expectation that professionals will be ethical. Should the voluntary controls of ethics be ineffective, law and other regulatory mechanisms may have to narrow the area of freedom of choice left to professionals, and this will in turn limit how decent professionals can exercise their judgment.

Actually, we might well talk of three systems of regulating professional conduct: (a) professional autonomy constrained only by ethics and the operation of the market system, (b) governmental regulation by the legal system, or (c) organizational regulation by the professional associations. The choice between what spheres of professional practice should be subject to each type of regulation is a critical question that cannot be answered solely as a matter of theory. Given the different sanctions, procedures for evaluation, and consequences of breach, the territory governed by each of the three systems depends on what the contemporary problems of professional practice are and how they should be dealt with.

The organized professions have resisted leaving the regulation of professional practice either exclusively to the law or solely to the private ethics of practitioners. Professional groups wish to retain substantial regulatory power in order to monitor how professionals function. If they label this area one of professional ethics, they have grounds to argue that the law should only narrowly concern itself with professional activity and leave regulation to professional associations. If they relegate the area of professional practice to pure ethics, they lose their justification for regulating and monitoring the way professionals practice.

It is to the self-interest of individual practitioners to desire the widest range of autonomy, thus leaving the regulation of their activities free of external controls, except the economic one of the market. This interest in wide autonomy could be based either on greed, that is, the freedom of the individual market performer to make as much money as possible, or else on the desire of decent people to be free of bureaucratic controls in order to perform services in creative and socially useful ways.

The self-interest of the client, the consumer, might be to have stronger governmental regulation of professionals. Redress for damage caused by unethical activity is more likely to be achieved. It is the one regulatory system that nonprofessionals can influence. One caveat is that if professional autonomy produces better practitioners and they operate in general in an ethical way, the interest of consumers would be furthered by encouraging autonomy.

If one considers the profession as a separate organization from individual members and with different goals from those individuals, it is to the self-interest of the professional association to have strong regulatory power, in order to decide who qualifies to join the profession's monopoly of expertise and how that expertise is used. It is the organized profession that formulates the formal code of ethics, retains the power to amend or change it, and exercises powerful influence on how it is taught in the professional schools.[19] Professional ethics as a concept is closely tied with the interests of the organized profession. One of its roles may well be to retain power in the professional group by denying genuine autonomy to nonconventional professionals and at the same time denying real regulatory power to the legal system. Closely connected with this is the role of professional ethics as public relations, persuading the general public and the profession's clientele that governmental regulation is not necessary because professionals will deal with the problems.

Apart from this political role of protecting the regulatory monopoly of the organized profession, professional ethics as an area of both teaching and scholarship has two quite different tasks. One is to lay down the limits on how the profession should be practiced and this is essentially a law-type activity. The second is to model and influence the creation of professional character so that the exercise of discretion and judgment will be done in ways that are decent and responsible. This latter belongs clearly to the field of ethics. These two objectives or projects are not necessarily incompatible, but require such different attitudes that they cannot be effectively taught together in a single course.

NOTES

1. One well-known debate about this issue was between H.L.A. Hart and Lon Fuller. See Hart, "Positivism and the Separation of Law and Morals," 71 HARV. L. REV. 593 (1958), and "Positivism and Fidelity to Law—A Reply to Professor Hart," 71 HARV. L. REV. 630 (1958). This debate continued in H.L.A. Hart, THE CONCEPT OF LAW (Oxford, Clarendon Press), 1961, and Lon Fuller, THE MORALITY OF LAW (New Haven: Yale University Press, 1964). Another famous dispute was between Justice Abe Fortas and Professor Howard Zinn over the legitimacy of civil disobedience in protesting the Vietnam War. Abe Fortas, CONCERNING DISSENT AND CIVIL DISOBEDIENCE (New York: New American Library, 1968), and Howard Zinn, DISOBEDIENCE AND DEMOCRACY: NINE FALLACIES ON LAW AND ORDER (New York, Random House, 1968).

2. A contemporary example is the argument made by prolife zealots charged with having murdered obstetricians who are performing abortions. They contend they are obeying God's law and that taking one life to save many other innocent ones is justifiable homicide. Such arguments have not been given credence in the courts. See "Killer of Abortion Doctor Is Sentenced to Die," NEW YORK TIMES (Wednesday, December 7, 1994): A16.

3. See Katharine Q. Seelye, "Packwood Resigns Senate Seat after Panel Details Evidence," NEW YORK TIMES (Friday, September 8, 1995): p. A1, col. 6.

4. Stuart Hampshire, "Public and Private Morality," in PUBLIC AND PRIVATE MORALITY, Stuart Hampshire, ed. (Cambridge, Cambridge University Press, 1978), p. 33.

5. There is an interesting discussion of law's formality in Stanley Fish, THERE'S NO SUCH THING AS FREE SPEECH . . . AND IT'S A GOOD THING TOO (New York: Oxford University Press, 1994), Chapter 11.

6. On the question of whether there is an ethical duty, cf. T. M. Scanlon, "Rights, Goals and Fairness," in PUBLIC AND PRIVATE MORALITY, Stuart Hampshire, ed. (Cambridge: Cambridge University Press, 1978), pp. 110–111, where he says:

[in considering] our apparent policy regarding mutual aid. If, as seems to be the case, we are prepared to allow a person to fail to save another when doing so would involve a moderately heavy sacrifice, why not allow him to do the same for the sake of a much greater benefit, to be gained from that person's death? The answer seems to be that, while a principle of mutual aid giving less consideration to the donor's sacrifice strikes us as too demanding, it is not nearly as threatening as a policy allowing one to consider the benefits to be gained from a person's death.

See also the discussion in Ronald Dworkin, TAKING RIGHTS SERIOUSLY (Cambridge, Mass.; Harvard University Press, 1978), p. 99.

7. 3 Pick. 207 (Mass., 1826).

8. H.L.A. Hart, "Positivism and the Separation of Law and Morals," 71 HARV. L. REV. 597–598 (1958).

9. This difference is one of degree rather than kind between the two systems. Ronald Dworkin has argued persuasively that "principles" and "policies" describe most legal standards in the way they operate better than do "rules." See Chapter 2, "The Model of Rules I," in Dworkin, TAKING RIGHTS SERIOUSLY.

10. This distinction may help explain the irreconcilabilities over abortion. Prolife people argue from an ethics perspective where taking an absolute position makes sense. Prochoice people take a legal stance where one must permit more freedom and allow for a variety of circumstances,which would affect the question of whether to impose legal sanctions. Prolife theorists evade the issue of appropriate sanctions for abortion.

11. For a discussion of this level of expectation of professional performance, see Banks McDowell, "The Ethical Obligations of Professional Teachers (of Ethics), PROFESSIONAL ETHICS: A MULTIDISCIPLINARY JOURNAL, Vol. 1, Nos. 3 & 4 (Fall/Winter 1992): 58–59.

12. O. W. Holmes, Jr., "The Path of the Law," 10 HARVARD LAW REVIEW 457 (1897), p. 459: "If you want to know the law and nothing else, you must look at it as a bad man, who cares only for the material consequences which such knowledge enables him to predict, not as a good one, who finds his reasons for conduct, whether inside the law or outside of it, in the vaguer sanctions of conscience."

13. This is an insight J. L. Austin had when he suggested that one of the great sources for studying excuses was the law. See J. L. Austin, "A Plea for Excuses," PHILOSOPHICAL PAPERS, 3d ed. (Oxford: Oxford University Press, 1979), pp. 187–188.

14. This statement is too absolute to be empirically true. In difficult cases, the court has a number of ways of evading troublesome questions and postponing decision, but the court will always appear to decide the question before it.

15. This statement is less true of contemporary law because of the development of concepts of absolute liability and the use of liability insurance, where insurance pools rather than the actor's assets are used for compensation.

16. This dilemma between the drive for financial success and the ideal of service, which underlies the concept of professionalism, was the subject of an earlier book, Banks McDowell, ETHICAL CONDUCT AND THE PROFESSIONAL'S DILEMMA: CHOOSING BETWEEN SERVICE AND SUCCESS (Westport, Conn.: Quorum Books, 1991).

17. Andre Brink, "The Writer as Witch," in THE DISSIDENT WORD: THE OXFORD AMNESTY LECTURES 1995, Christ Miller, ed. (New York: Basic Books, 1996).

18. A good discussion of the importance of judgment in professional ethics and ways in which it might be taught can be found in David Luban and Michael Millemann, 9 GEORGETOWN JOURNAL OF LEGAL ETHICS 31 (1995).

19. I first met this observation in Robert Paul Wolff's book, THE IDEAL OF THE UNIVERSITY (Boston: Beacon Press, 1969), where he argues that the university is perverted by the presence of professional schools who are more controlled by and responsive to the professions than to the academy and to academic standards and values. Almost anyone who has taught in a professional school knows of this ongoing conflict between whether the professional teacher is an academic or a professional with competing pulls from each direction.

5

Defenses: The Legal Excuses

My principal interest is in excuses that are given in response to claims that the (professional) actor was unethical in some particular context. Unless one adopts the position that professional ethics are really law so that defenses rather than excuses would be the appropriate way to avoid responsibility, a discussion of legal defenses has relevance only in the ways it might shed light on how ethical excuses should operate. Legal defenses are not discussed here in great detail, but only those aspects raising important issues for ethics theory. Ethics in general and professional ethics in particular may learn both from the way legal duties are defined and then may be avoided by defenses.

Before discussing particular defenses, two important matters need clarification: (1) the way the elements of duty, breach, causation, damage, and responsibility interrelate with defenses, and (2) the relationship between the various legal sanctions that might be imposed and the likelihood a defense will be accepted.

Lawyers know that the overriding issue in litigation is legal responsibility. Their task during a trial if they represent the plaintiff (or the prosecution) is to establish responsibility; if they represent the defendant, to deny responsibility. The plaintiff's lawyer must establish the existence of the duty, the breach by defendant, damage to the victim, and a causal relationship between breach and damage. If necessary, the defendant introduces defenses. The secondary task of plaintiff's lawyer is to rebut any claims of legal defenses. The secondary task, and often the dominant task, of defendant's lawyer is to rebut the elements of duty, breach, damage, or causation.

In all litigation, these elements overlap and interweave, but most arguments by the defense attorney are directed to denying the affirmative elements of liability. How much does practical ethics take, or should take, the same approach? Since the focus is on the legal equivalent of ethical excuses, I try not to let the discussion spill over into areas of duty and breach, but that is not always possible. For example, is lack of causal connection between defendant's acts and plaintiff's injury a matter of duty, breach, or legal defense?[1] That issue crops up several times in the following discussion.

The second point to be understood is that a trial has two separate phases. The first answers the question: did the defendant act illegally? A subsidiary question is: into which particular category of wrongdoing (having different elements and calling for different sanctions) did the wrongful act fit? Once it is determined that the defendant acted illegally, the second stage decides what sanction should attach to the wrongful act. The law allows substantial flexibility in the sanction, but there are outer limits and usually lower limits for a particular wrongdoing. Lawyers, and their clients, tend to regard this second phase as more important.[2] For most people today, the consequences of wrongdoing, that is, the price they must pay, is their principal concern.

While the question of whether defendant acted illegally is analytically separate from the question of what the sanction should be, the judge and jury are usually aware of the range of potential penalties. They let their view of the appropriateness of the punishment in relation to the nature of the breach affect the decision whether there was wrongdoing or not, as well as whether the wrongdoing belongs in a more severe or milder category of illegality. While the law is often concerned with avoidance defenses, it is frequently interested in mitigating defenses that control the type and amount of sanction.

Lawyers are just as captivated by the two-person model as are ethicists. For the lawyer, it is plaintiff and defendant. Lawyers analyze and resolve the most complex social issues, including constitutional law disputes that define the very structure of society, as if they were simple litigation between two parties. This method of analysis makes problems understandable and manageable, but it can also produce distortions. Social problems are not just a summation of a host of individual problems.

Since law is more restricted in coverage and harsher in its consequences than ethics, one might think any excuse that works as a legal defense would automatically qualify as an ethical justification. As we discuss the defenses, one recurring question will be whether a particular legal defense is an ethical justification. Not always. For example, we might feel a mistake was enough to excuse legal responsibility, but sufficiently caused by carelessness or indifference so the actor should be ethically responsible for her conduct.

The important legal defenses are the following. Unless necessary, I will not separate the criminal from the civil defenses. Most defenses are available both in criminal and civil trials.

ACCIDENT

"It was an accident" is a common reaction, excuse, or evasion used by someone accused of being responsible for damage done to another. While we frequently use "accident," we seldom have a precise idea of its meaning. It could mean "I did not intend to do it," " I did not expect it to happen," "I did it through carelessness," "I made a mistake," "I could not have avoided it," or "I had nothing to do with it."

J. L. Austin suggested that in ordinary language "it was an accident" is often confused with "it was a mistake." In a footnote, he has a marvelous little story illustrating the confusion and distinguishing the two:

> You have a donkey, so have I, and they graze in the same field. The day comes when I conceive a dislike for mine. I go to shoot it, draw a bead on it, fire: the brute falls in its tracks. I inspect the victim, and find to my horror that it is *your* donkey. I appear on your doorstep with the remains and say— what? "I say, old sport, I'm awfully sorry, &c., I've shot your donkey *by accident*? Or *by mistake*?" Then again, I go to shoot my donkey as before, draw a bead on it, fire—but as I do so, the beasts move, and to my horror yours falls. Again the scene on the doorstep—what do I say? "By mistake"? Or "by accident"?[3]

Lawyers admit both accident and mistake as defenses, but accord them different weight. Mistake, which will be discussed in the next section, is sometimes a defense; unavoidable accident, if established, almost always is. Why the difference?

First, we need to clear up a confusion between two quite different meanings of "accident," used by both laypeople and lawyers. We all commonly use the unqualified term for a class of cases where there is legal, and, quite possibly, ethical liability. The best example is the automobile "accident." What is being described here are acts of negligence, that is, events that could have been prevented by the use of reasonably prudent care. Accident functions only as a mitigating excuse or defense in such cases. If the act were intentional, rather than negligent, the sanction would be more severe. If it were a true accident, rather than an occurrence caused by negligence, there would be no sanction at all. Because I am primarily concerned with exculpatory or avoidance excuses, "accident" will be used to mean "unavoidable accident," rather than negligence. When lawyers talk about defenses, they use that term. This is defined by the Restatement of Torts, Second as follows:

> The words "unavoidable accident" are used throughout the restatement of this Subject to denote the fact that the harm which is so described is not caused by any tortious act of the one whose conduct is in question.[4]

This may strike nonlawyers as circular. It is an unavoidable accident if you are not liable, and you are not liable if it is an unavoidable accident. There is, however, a legal process by which liability is determined. In that process it is necessary to determine whether the defendant has caused the injury and could have foreseen it.

In order for an accident to be classed as unavoidable, it has to be an occurrence that was not intended by the actor and which, under the circumstances, could not have been foreseen or prevented by the exercise of reasonable precautions.[5] An example of an avoidable accident, that is, legal negligence, is where because of excessive speed or inattention, an automobile crash occurs. An unavoidable accident would be a crash where the driver suddenly loses control of the car through a heart attack, a stroke, or an epileptic fit. Crashing the automobile then was not intentional, foreseeable, or controllable. If the driver knew, however, that he was likely to have such an attack, he might be negligent in driving at all and thus could be liable. Another common example of unavoidable accident is when a pedestrian runs out in front of a car and the driver has no time in which to avoid hitting him.

The strongest meaning of accident is that no human actor was responsible. The event or happening, labeled an unavoidable accident, is almost always abnormal and unusual so that a prudent person could not have anticipated the happening and acted to prevent it. Chance, nature, God, or other nonhuman agency may be credited with "responsibility" for the occurrence, but not an identifiable human being.

In what context of professional liability is the defense of accident available and likely to be used? When the professional is accused of acting with less than adequate competence, in other words, the malpractice action. The result of the professional's services is less than was promised to, expected by, or satisfactory to the client. The professional, who claims the result was an unavoidable accident, may well be saying that he could not have foreseen the consequences nor could he have prevented them from occurring by the use of ordinary professional care. These issues are at the heart of most malpractice actions.

In fixing liability and the consequent sanctions, the law is restricted to activities that can be legitimately allocated to the responsibility of a particular human being. If one cannot fix blame because of unforeseeability or lack of control of the occurrence, there should be no legal liability. Should ethics take the same position? One might argue that, given the less damaging sanctions in ethics, we could on occasion apportion ethical blame for accidental happenings when there is no legal blame. This can occur because matters are never as black and white as theory would indicate. There will be many cases where extraordinary care by a human might have prevented the occurrence. Since the law seldom requires extraordinary care, they would label such occurrences as accidents. Ethics could insist on extraordinary care in many contexts when the law does not.

In the practical world in which the law has to function, it is not always easy to tell whether a human being could have avoided what has been labeled an accident by being more cautious or acting more defensively. The law in situations of doubt may refuse to allocate responsibility to that individual for the damage. In a system of ethics where the only consequence of an avoidable accident would be nonmaterial sanctions, such as blame or loss of respect, ethicists might be more willing than lawyers to ascribe responsibility.

The concept of accident precludes it from being used as an affirmative cause of action so there would be no attempt to define the concept in the same way that theories that are both affirmative and defensive, such as fraud or consent, have been defined. There is one context, however, where lawyers have struggled with the definition of accident. Since an accident is unexpected and to some extent unforeseeable, it is an occurrence that one should be able to insure against. Accident insurance has been available for a long time. Lawyers drafting such insurance policies have to define the coverage, that is, what is an accident insurers are willing to accept the risk for. "An accident within accident insurance policies is an event happening without any human agency, or, if happening through such agency, an event which, under circumstances, is unusual and not expected by the person to whom it happens."[6] Such defining clauses often required that the loss be caused by accidental means, rather than being just an accidental result. It was also common to require that the loss be caused solely and exclusively by such external means, attempting to exclude losses that were caused, in part, by nonaccidental means, such as disease.[7]

What the insurance company drafters are trying to do with such definitions is to exclude either extremely rash activity that is likely to produce injury or the "moral hazard" of intentionally injuring oneself or claiming such an injury in order to recover on the policy. The consequences of such action are not unexpected or random, but clearly foreseeable, if not expected. This would upset the randomness of events on which actuarial science can make predictions and on which insurance premiums are predicated. Definitions designed to preclude such possibilities would not necessarily be good guides to what kinds of events should be labeled accidents as defenses against tort liability.

For lawyers, the notion of accident is closely tied to the concept of causation. In almost all crimes and torts, an essential element is that the defendant's action "caused" the injury.[8] Without the requisite causal connection between the defendant's act and the injury to the plaintiff, there is no legal responsibility and thus we label the event an accident. When one pleads accident as a defense, this is not very different from pleading lack of causation.

A fundamental difficulty in understanding how lawyers define and apply accident is they use a functional approach, controlled by both context and underlying public policies in the law of tort. The concept can be applied broadly or narrowly. If they want to attach responsibility for a result on a particular person, they cannot label the event an accident, or at least an unavoidable accident. There are competing purposes in tort law (and perhaps in criminal law as well). One is to compensate the victim for injuries. The other is to fix fault and punish the wrongdoer. Depending on which is seen as dominant, the concept of accident will be narrow, allowing for a wider set of cases where victims receive compensation, or broad, fixing responsibility only in clear cases of fault, causation, and responsibility. In recent decades, tort law has emphasized the purpose of providing compensation for victims. Thus accident is less available as a defense than it would have been earlier. This narrowing of the number of events labeled as accidents can create problems in the element of responsibility and particularly, with ethical responsibility.

In modern industrial society, neither the family nor tight-knit communities adequately perform the function of caring for injured persons either in the short run or, in case of severe accidents, in the long run. There is enormous pressure to transfer the cost and care of people injured in "accidents" to either government and governmental insurance programs, or through the law to individual wrongdoers and behind them their private insurance carriers. Such a social policy makes accident a less effective and fashionable defense than it used to be. This illustrates the function of excuses in defining, broadening, or narrowing other concepts in responsibility, such as duty.

Does this practice of transferring "accidental" losses to the responsibility of someone in order to award victims compensation have an effect on ethical analysis? Are we today in the zone of ethics less inclined to let losses be the product of chance or to assume responsibility for our own misfortunes? Are we now conditioned, when we are accused of unethical action, to look for and say it must be somebody else's fault?

There are two quite different questions about the use of accident in relation to ethical excuses. The first is whether we should accept accident as an ethical excuse. The answer is clearly yes, but in more restricted fashion than the law. The second and more important question is whether the influence of ethics should be used to minimize the number of accidents. Should we emphasize an ethical duty to act with greater care (less negligence)? To the extent we have narrowed the use of accident in defense of legal claims for compensation for victims, there is a greater need for individual actors to minimize their careless or inattentive actions. The tort system cannot carry the cost of too heavy a welfare burden. The prevention of growing carelessness cannot, however, be totally achieved inside the legal system by increasing sanctions. Tort sanctions are not being used to minimize conscious conduct, but to transfer losses to achieve welfare objectives.

MISTAKE

This is the defense that J. L. Austin thought was often confused with accident. In a criminal proceeding, if the actor proceeds on a mistaken belief that certain facts exist and his action would have been legal on those facts, the mistake could be a legal defense. A mistake as to the state of the law may also be a defense.[9]

If two parties make a contract based on an assumed set of facts that later turns out to have been different from the reality, the courts may find there was no contract and thus no obligation on either side. An example is the old Michigan case of *Sherwood v. Walker*,[10] which has delighted and perplexed generations of American law students. The defendant was a cattle breeder who agreed to sell a pure-bred Angus cow, named Rose 2d of Aberlone, to plaintiff for $80. Both parties assumed she was barren and was only good for slaughter. If not barren, she would be worth $750 to $1,000. After the contract was agreed to, it was discovered she was with calf. When the seller refused to deliver Rose, the buyer sued to recover possession. The Supreme Court of Michigan decided in favor of the seller. That court said it was a clear general rule that a party who consented to a contract could refuse to perform if it was based on a mistake of a material fact. The mistake must be mutual, that is, shared by both parties, and must be substantial going to the identity of the subject matter of the contract, not to its quality or value. It is necessary for the law of contract not to allow mistakes of value or quality of goods sold to be a defense. When a party becomes dissatisfied and tries to repudiate the contract, it is usually because he was mistaken as to the true value of the subject matter. If such a defense were accepted, few contracts would have any binding quality. The buyer contended there was no mistake as to identity because they both intended the same cow, but the court said: "A barren cow is substantially a different creature than a breeding one."

The law of contract has always distinguished between mutual and unilateral mistake. In the case of mutual mistake, both parties operate under a misapprehension. Both were, if you will, careless and did not adequately protect themselves. Why should we let a party, who was mistaken, profit through the use of the courts against another party also mistaken? Unilateral mistake, where only one party was in error, is not a defense unless the mistake produces an offer so clearly in error that no reasonable party could believe it was a genuine offer.[11] Then we are back to both parties being at fault, one making a mistake and the other intentionally trying to take advantage of it.

Mistake shows that for careful analysis defenses should be related to the particular duty that has been breached and the underlying policies behind that duty. Mistake in criminal law is a defense, but judges and juries may be dubious about finding it. Mistake is theoretically a defense because punishment as a deterrent makes little sense if the person was mistaken about the facts. While mistake might be a defense in a criminal trial, it could well not be a defense in an action in tort to recover civil damages because the underlying policy here is not deterrence, but compensation for the victim. Mistake in contract is more likely to be a defense because the obligation depends on consent and consent depends on knowing the context under which the obligation has been assumed.

If we return to the confusion that J. L. Austin thought might exist as to whether the excuse given was mistake or accident, do they have equal force as defenses or excuses? We feel that mistakes can be minimized by the exercise of care, sometimes extraordinary care, so that the human being need not make mistakes, even though we all do. On the other hand, none of us can prevent the happening of an accident, which by definition is unforeseeable and thus unavoidable.

LACK OF INTENT

The law recognizes lack of mental capacity as a defense and usually requires the element of intentionality. These are two related, but distinct defenses or reasons why an actor should not be legally responsible. Since both refer to the actor's state of mind, I analyze them together.

One form of this defense is where the actor lacks the minimum mental capacity to be responsible for his acts. This has been most discussed in connection with the insanity defense in criminal law. Anglo-American law has never in modern times taken the position that all persons whatever their mental capacity should be responsible for their acts. One exemption is very young children. Another are people so insane they have no understanding of the nature of their acts and that what they are doing is wrong. The major debate has not been about whether lack of capacity to understand should be a defense, but where to draw the line between competency and incompetency.

This threshold requirement of minimum competence for legal responsibility flows from a feeling that it is unjust to punish someone who did not have the capacity to choose to act in the legal or proper way. Legal liability should not be imposed on someone who is not sufficiently rational to understand the situation he is in and what his available options are. The purpose of the criminal law is not merely to punish for the past acts, but to deter future wrongful action. A perpetrator incapable of being rational cannot be deterred. Of course, one might argue that deterrence is not aimed solely or primarily at the offender, but at others who may learn from his example. But causing someone to suffer just to educate others seems to offend our sense of justice.

The civil law, as distinguished from the criminal law, is concerned with corrective justice, a transfer of the goods from the defendant to the injured plaintiff to restore a just balance. The justification for that transfer is the defendant's wrongdoing. If he was not competent enough to avoid the activity or know that he should have done so, we do not consider him as acting with sufficient fault to justify such a transfer.

Even when actors are above the threshold level of competence so they can be legally responsible, lawyers have always stressed the importance of the element of intention. This is not primarily a matter of good or bad motive. Rather, it is to determine whether the actor could have foreseen the consequences of his action and ought to bear responsibility for them. The law is hesitant about transferring losses from an actor who neither chose the action nor foresaw the consequences to a person who suffered harm. In the criminal law, this element of intention is the *mens rea*, the intent to do a criminal act. In torts or civil wrongs, it is the intent to do harm to a person or her property. In contracts, it is the intent to make a promise and assume a promissory obligation. The specific intent required will vary from the criminal law to torts and from torts to contract. The differences are produced by the policies underlying these separate legal categories and those distinctions between the various categories have little application to ethics.

When discussing intention, we are moving into the realm of motivation, subjective states, foreseeability, reasoning processes, all aspects that are difficult to prove and to define. One might expect lawyers, a practical group of professionals and well aware of the difficulties of fact-finding in this area, to eschew using intention at all. There are, however, important distinctions between those acts to be condemned on the one hand and legal or acceptable acts on the other that can be made only by using these subjective factors. For example, assault requires an intent to do bodily harm. This element is necessary to distinguish illegal invasions of bodily integrity from the casual touching or bumping that close physical proximity often makes unavoidable. As we move into the most serious forms of assault, those that lead to death, intention becomes even more critical. It is premeditation that distinguishes capital or first-degree murder from second-degree murder, where anger or passion instantaneously produced the act, and then on down to the lesser offense of manslaughter caused by carelessness. Another example of the importance of intention is fraud, which requires an intent to deceive. This is necessary to distinguish casual or unimportant misstatements from those lies for which the legal system imposes responsibility.

This claim of lack of intent might well not be thought of as a defense, but rather the denial of an essential element of legal duty or obligation. Most legal causes of action, except negligence, require a finding of intentionality or a special state of mind as an element of the duty. This "defense" could be treated as a denial of that element.

SELF-DEFENSE (SELF-PROTECTION)

The obvious instance of self-protection as a defense against legal responsibility is self-defense in criminal law. One can protect his own person and property from criminal activity by using the minimum necessary force. There are interesting subissues about what constitutes minimum necessary force in the particular context and whether if one can escape from an attack, that is required before taking the other's life. A modern variant of this matter is the "battered woman syndrome." There has been much discussion in recent decades about whether a woman who had been consistently abused by a brutal man can take his life in defense or should, or realistically could, have escaped.

There is an interesting problem, both in theory and in practice, about what constitutes the person to be protected. As a first-year law student, I was intrigued by an old English case, which held that striking a person's sword, horse, or walking stick would constitute a battery against the person. Clearly, there are areas outside the skin that seem to be a part of the person, at least psychologically. This includes some property, particularly unique and intimate personal items, and may also include other persons, like members of one's immediate family. The law has struggled with how far beyond protection of one's physical person the immunity from legal responsibility goes when one is engaged in protecting one's (expanded) self. Can he use physical force in protecting members of his family from attack by other persons and his property from damage or theft? The law has generally answered yes, with the qualification that only reasonable force can be used.[12]

How much beyond protection against direct assault or trespass does this defense carry? Threats to the person are not merely physical. Perhaps the best protection against threats from others is to amass sufficient wealth and power to deter others from trying to take advantage. Clearly the law does not in general require an actor to subordinate his or her interests to those of another party, or to be altruistic. A classic illustration, discussed above, causing ethical difficulty for some first-year torts students is the problem of the duty to save or assist others in danger. If I see a person drowning in the lake, I am not under any legal duty to spend my time or place myself in danger to attempt to save the person. In fact, if I make the attempt and do it badly, I may be legally liable to the victim for my negligence.

What lies behind this defense is the ticklish and fundamental legal and ethical problem of whether and when an actor should subordinate his own interests to that of others. Saving another person whose life is in danger often places the rescuer's life at an equal risk. Should the law compel everyone to try to be a hero? Our individualistic and capitalist society has placed the importance of self-preferring actions, such as ambition and drive for personal gain, near the top of the hierarchy of political and economic values. At the same time, we value altruistic actions. We are, however, inclined to leave those to the personal choice of the individual actor, who is free to be charitable or as indifferent to the interests of others as he chooses. Neither ethics nor law at the present time gives much, if any, guidance to how one should make the choices between self-interest and altruism.[13]

There are some relationships, however, where the cultural and legal choice weights the duty to others above that of self-interest. The most obvious is between family members, such as the responsibility of a parent to a child or of spouses to each other.[14]

In addition to family, other relationships, where one party is expected to subordinate its self-interest to the interests of others, are fiduciary—beneficiary and professional—client. The professional is explicitly expected to subordinate his interests to those of the client, if there is a conflict. Obviously that subordination is not total. If a professional must choose between caring for a sick child or performing a duty to a client, most people and the law would in many contexts accept that as a defense. It raises the interesting problem, when the claims of a member of the professional's family and the claims of a client conflict, how these competing interests ought to be ranked.

VICTIM'S RESPONSIBILITY

In this section, I lump together several legal defenses, contributory negligence, provocation, and the "clean hands" doctrine in equity. All have as their underlying basis the argument that it was really the victim who was responsible, or at least more responsible, for the damage. This is related to the ethical excuse "blaming the victim," considered in Chapter 3, but represents those situations where the law has decided the loss really was more the victim's responsibility than the defendant's.

There has always been a strong policy in the law that the injured party should be innocent and bear no causal responsibility for the damage before he is entitled to invoke the assistance of the legal system. Since civil litigation is intended to transfer loss from one party to another on the basis of fault, it is important that the transferee's fault be less than that of the party who would have to make the transfer.

If the victim provoked the action, usually a physical attack, he should not be able to recover in damages nor should there be criminal liability. There has been substantial litigation about what constitutes provocation. Provocation must be defined in terms of the duty of acceptable social intercourse and what a person must tolerate before she is entitled to react in self-protection. Words, however insulting, are generally not sufficient to justify a physical assault. On the other hand, an assault would justify a reaction in self-defense.

The defense of contributory negligence requires the plaintiff bringing a negligence action to establish that he was not himself negligent or, if so, that the negligence did not contribute to the result in any way. In many jurisdictions, tort law has now adopted comparative negligence, which permits plaintiff to recover even if his negligence partially caused the injury. Many of those states restrict recovery to parties whose negligence contributed less than 50 percent to the injury. The requirement of plaintiff's innocence has moved from complete to partial.

A third instance is the "clean hands" doctrine in equity jurisprudence. Equitable remedies will not be granted in favor of a party who has acted in an inequitable manner and thus cannot be said to come into court with clean hands herself.

One element discussed in Chapter 2 that is a central component of responsibility for lawyers is *causation*. The question is whether the action of the defendant can be said to be the cause of the injury to the victim. If the victim provoked the action, then the victim's actions were the real cause of the injury.

This makes the defense of provocation closely related to the excuse of blaming the victim, discussed and dismissed in Chapter 3 on ethical excuses. There are two points to be made in comparing the legal defense with the ethical excuse. In law, the validity of the defense is determined by objective third persons, the judge and jury, and they must find that the victim is really the responsible party for his own injury. While their decision may reflect the stereotypical biases of the society against disfavored groups, they will not share individual or personal animosities, so the problem of rationalization by the actor, which is a serious one in ethical excuses, is not as involved here. The second point of comparison is that an ethical system, and most particularly a professional ethical system, can and should have as a purpose the eradication of stereotypical or personal biases by the actor and by the persons occupying judgmental roles in the legal system.

This policy of requiring relative innocence of the victim has weakened in tort since the development of liability insurance. The judge and jury are not now weighing the question of whether we should require the defendant to transfer his assets to compensate a plaintiff who may herself not be without fault. The question presently is whether a third-party insurer should pay for the injuries to the plaintiff and that has certainly minimized the question of relative balance of fault.

FRAUD (MISREPRESENTATION)

Fraud is a well-recognized ground of legal liability, an affirmative cause of action. If one makes a statement of fact that is untrue, knowing that it is untrue, with the intent to commit fraud, and another person relies on that statement to her detriment, there may be both criminal liability and civil liability in tort. Fraud is that subclass of lying or misrepresentation that gives rise to legal remedies. Fraud may also operate, however, as a defense, particularly in contract, where the promisor who is being sued alleges she was induced to make the promise or enter the contract by fraudulent statements made by the plaintiff.

Although this is an area where the same concept is both an affirmative cause of action and a defense, there are differences between its content in the two uses. Fraud as an affirmative cause of action requires what the lawyers call *scienter*, the intention to mislead through a false statement. In contract, an "innocent" misrepresentation, that is, one made without intent to defraud, can operate as a defense.[15] Why should there be a difference in elements in the affirmative and the defensive concept? When it is used defensively, it leaves the parties in *status quo*; that is, no transfer will be made from defendant to plaintiff. That result can be justified solely on the basis of a false statement made knowingly but without intent to deceive. If the victim transferred something to the defrauder, the court can order that object or the financial equivalent to be restored, thus returning the parties to the *status quo ante*, the situation they were in before the fraud. Transferring a loss from the plaintiff to the defendant, which would be the purpose of an affirmative action for fraud, requires a higher level of wrongdoing or fault.

Fraud as a defense could have been discussed in the preceding section under a broader notion of victim's responsibility or those situations where the alleged victim rather than the actor was at fault. It is, however, a common problem, closely related to ethical discussions arising out of lying. Fraud is that subclass of false statements so serious and so damaging that the law will attempt to suppress it and will protect the victims. It deserves separate and more thorough discussion.

Today, it is assumed that fraud is widespread particularly in making claims against insurance companies and in making claims against government agencies, either in case of social insurance schemes, such as Medicare and Social Security, or against the Federal Emergency Management Agency in emergency situations, such as floods and earthquakes. Whenever a questionable claim against such an institutional defendant is denied, the common defense is to argue that the claim is fraudulent. This may be grounded on the belief that there was no loss or that the amount of loss claimed is exaggerated.

In the two-person model of ethical theory or the simple person-to-person relationships of an earlier time, widespread fraud would not be expected because of relational factors and the greater possibility of knowledge of the misrepresenter by the "victim," so that the trust that fraud depends on would less likely be given to dishonest persons. In the complex, highly mobile, and more alienated modern world, such factors that would normally restrain the defrauder and cause the actor to be less hesitant about believing a particular person are not present, so we must be more cynical and less trusting in all our dealings. This may mean that many professionals and professional associations are viewed now more like insurance companies and government agencies, that is, as groups ripe for fraudulent activity. Professionals, particularly those assumed to be wealthy, such as medical doctors, may be subject to fraudulent activity by clients and thus would want to raise the defense in cases where claims for money damage are made against them.

DURESS OR NECESSITY

Duress and necessity are defenses in both criminal and civil law. Duress is compelling someone to do something they do not wish to do. Necessity is the use of another's property to save one's own property or life. Since I want to compare them with the ethical excuse of irresistible pressure, I will lump them together as defenses that say the actor was compelled to act in the way he did. Those acts one is forced to do are not free or voluntary acts and thus are not a justifiable basis for imposing legal liability. A major difficulty is in defining what constitutes duress. Physical force that cannot be successfully resisted is clearly duress. The paradigm example is where someone put a pistol to my head and said he would shoot me unless I signed a contract. If I signed as a consequence of that threat, the contract is invalid. It certainly does not represent free choice. Likewise, if someone physically stronger than I seized my hand and forced me to sign my name by controlling its movements with the pen, there is no contract.

This raises an old problem in legal (and moral) theory. If someone points a gun at me and says he will shoot me unless I kill a third party, may I kill the other person in order to save my own life? This defense was raised by Nazi concentration camp guards who claimed they would have lost their lives had they not participated in the Holocaust. This excuse may seem to be related to self-defense, but there it is only the life of the threatener that can be taken, not an innocent life. The defense of taking someone else's life in order to save one's own, though frequently raised, is rarely persuasive.[16] There are two issues. Could one really have escaped the pressure without taking another's life? The second is whether, given the supreme importance of life, I am justified in saving my own life at a cost of another innocent life.

A difficult issue for Anglo-American law has been the degree to which economic pressure should constitute duress. Most pressures we feel in modern life that force us to do things we would rather not are economic rather than physical. Yet in a capitalist view of human interaction, there is always an assumption, which is often counterfactual, that people enjoy sufficient equality in intellectual capacity, economic assets, educational background, and opportunity so that any contracts or other economic arrangements they make are considered to be bargains struck on a level playing field. This is probably a necessary assumption to make in order to administer a system of commercial law where reliance on bargains is critical. If a person could later raise the defense of economic duress, few contracts or other financial dealings could be relied on with certainty.

Even though the law has with reluctance and only in a limited way recognized economic duress as a legal defense, it is one of the most frequent ethical excuses offered by professionals to explain or justify why they act unethically. In the economic arena, which is, of course, where professional activity belongs, the motivations for all activity including unethical activity would normally be economic pressure or the hope of economic reward. The most important and difficult role for professional ethics is to put some constraints on the drive to amass economic wealth and power at all costs.

Why is the law reluctant to use economic duress or necessity as a defense? In our political and economic theory, we prefer to leave the economic domain as an area of freedom or autonomy for the participants in order to encourage productivity, flexibility and inventiveness. The regulation of such activities by the law tends to be somewhat heavy-handed and invasive. This preference for freedom in commercial activity is also thought to require wide protection of private property, which leads to very limited use of the doctrine of necessity. If economic actors wish to remain free from social or governmental regulation, they ought to be more concerned with acting with sufficient ethical restraint in their relationships with others so that the need for social and legal intervention will be minimized.

CONSENT

Consent from the victim, usually given in advance, excuses conduct that would be illegal without it. This is true, for instance, in assault and battery and explains why the kind of activity that occurs in boxing rings, in hockey rinks, or on football fields is not illegal. By participating in such games knowing their nature, each player consents to being manhandled in a way that would normally constitute tortious, if not criminal, activity. It also explains why surgeons, who have obtained consent from patients, can perform the most extreme sorts of physical intrusion on a body without legal liability, provided, of course, that they are not negligent. Merely signing a consent form where substantial psychological pressure is placed on a patient before an operation has become a formality and is not enough. The consent must be genuine based on full information about the operation and the risks. It certainly does not ever authorize careless or negligent behavior.

In the commercial field, consent, that is the foundation of contracts, also legitimates activity that would otherwise be illegal. Without a lease, the "lessee" would be a trespasser. Without a contract of sale, the "buyer" of a car would be a car thief, and so on. In fact, the early English courts, followed by American judges, developed a curious doctrine built on this notion. If a converter, or thief, took and used property without permission, the owner could "waive the tort and sue in assumpsit," that is, treat the transaction as a sale rather than a trespass or conversion. Since the law presumes people are honest, implying a promise to buy the property turns the converter from a thief into an honest buyer.

The defense, of course, requires that the consent given be genuine, without compulsion, and with some understanding of the consequences of the choice. In the modern era with its power imbalances, use of standardized forms, and increased skill at manipulation, there are often serious questions of whether a formal consent is a real consent.

One context of serious discussion in recent decades in relationship to professional activity is the so-called "informed consent" given by patients to doctors who are performing invasive procedures, such as surgery. Of course, one could say that all consent should be informed before it counts as a defense, but consent by patients given to doctors is the area where these issues have been more thoroughly discussed. Presumably, any professional relying on the consent of the client to justify potentially harmful activity should be held to this same standard of information developed for doctors, rather than to the minimal requirements in commercial transactions between parties dealing at arm's length.

Consent after the illegal or unethical conduct can also be a defense. Then it will be treated as a waiver of the right to sue. Any settlement of a disputed claim is consent not to sue in exchange for some settlement amount to be paid for the consent.

TRANSFER OF RESPONSIBILITY

While it is not technically a defense, this is as frequently used in law as a way of avoiding legal responsibility as it is used to avoid ethical responsibility. In the legal system where it is necessary to resolve the question of who actually has responsibility and must take the consequences, this defense raises special problems. The way in which the law has chosen to deal with it is instructive in considering how to handle it as an ethical excuse.

A common incidence is where the defendant in a criminal trial contends that someone else, often an accomplice, was the party who actually committed the crime. The doctrine of complicity makes the defense in such situations something less than absolute. The legal defense is not actually so much a transfer of responsibility, but rather pointing the finger at someone else.

The practice of cocriminals blaming each other is used by prosecutors to get one accomplice to give evidence against another. This practice gives rise to serious administrative and ethical problems. A recent case in Canada, the Paul Bernardo trial, which was almost as notorious there as the O. J. Simpson trial in the United States, illustrates this context of the defense, its use by the prosecution as a means of getting a conviction, and the administrative difficulties. Paul Bernardo and his wife, Karla Homulka, were suspected of having kidnapped, raped, tortured, and killed two young girls. Karla claimed that she was forced into participating by her husband and that she was in fact a battered woman. In a plea bargain, the prosecution let her plead guilty to second-degree murder and she received a sentence of twelve years in prison. This was done in exchange for her testimony against her husband. Shortly after the plea bargain, it was discovered that there were videotapes made of the sexual assaults and maltreatment, but not of the murders themselves. The tapes seemed to show that Karla was an active and willing participant. Paul Bernardo was convicted of first-degree murder and sentenced to life imprisonment. At the time of the plea bargaining, the prosecution thought Karla was not so involved and that without her testimony, they might not get a conviction of Paul. This case illustrates the problems of duress placed on the accomplice to force the agreement, the question of the reliability of the testimony so obtained, and the elemental question of justice where two cocriminals equally responsible are given such different sentences. After the trial, there was enormous public outrage at the light sentence given Karla, and public petitions were gathered all over Canada to try to rescind the plea bargain.

In civil actions, this defense is the attempt of one joint tortfeasor to transfer the blame to the other. This may take the guise of causation analysis; that is, which one really caused the damage? Litigating such issues can be time-consuming and very difficult. To deal with this administrative nightmare, the law developed the joint tortfeasor doctrine, which says that when two or more parties contribute to the commission of a tort, they are individually and severally liable for all the damage.

This excuse will be raised because of the difficulty in factually identifying the responsible party when several actors are involved in a wrongful act. The general reaction of the legal system has been to adopt rules that make all participants liable, in order to avoid the administrative problems of establishing which one is the most responsible or the truly responsible party. The most extreme of these solutions is the felony-murder rule. When two or more actors are involved in committing a serious crime and in the course of the crime, one criminal kills an innocent person, the other actors are also guilty of murder. Before any of these responsibility-sharing rules can be invoked, there has to be sufficient connection of the particular party with the wrongdoing to make the application of such rules at all palatable.

CONCLUSION

There is value in considering the legal defenses in a book focusing on professional ethics and appropriate excuses thereunder. Because defenses are constantly being litigated and refined by lawyers when deciding whether they are valid in particular cases, legal excuses have been worked out in great detail over a long period of time. It is not that defenses developed by lawyers are different from excuses used in ethics. They track closely together. What is important is that lawyers are concerned with questions of how excuses should be applied in particular contexts, and the degree of weight that should be given to each in real human controversies. The distinctions lawyers have worked out may shed light by comparison on relatively unexplored areas of ethical excuses. It is always instructive to ask whether a legal defense would be a valid ethical excuse, and if not, why not.

Given the severe external consequences of breaking the law, one moral (or perhaps practical) limitation on legal norms is that they have to be limited to a kind of minimum morality that can be expected of every member of the society, whatever his or her individual characteristics and values. Ethical systems are free to develop guidelines that are more flexible, individualized, and cover areas of what are for the law matters of liberty free from coercion, but where substantial damage can be done by actors if they are not restrained by decency and moral principles. An area of enormous current interest illustrating this in the United States is the operation of the First Amendment, which gives journalists almost absolute freedom to print anything they know, particularly if it is true. Should they do so when the outcome is the destruction of lives without substantial public gain? If one collapses the realms of law and ethics, they are free to do so. That is, if one says that the law defines not only the legal realm of liberty, but how one is entitled as a matter of ethics to act within it, then the problem disappears for the journalist, but obviously not for the people who have been destroyed.

Contrasting ethical excuses and legal defenses indicates that the fundamental difference between law and ethics may perhaps be found in the duty element. Ethical guidelines or norms set higher, more demanding, and more individualized duty requirements. Do defenses fashioned by the legal system for universal and restricted obligations apply to this heightened and more demanding duty element? A thorough analysis or statement of duty requires including the area of coverage and the justifications for not complying. The same justifications for saying that this demanding ethical duty does not exist in a particular context may not apply to whatever legal duties are imposed in the same context. This is not a theoretical matter, but one that has to be worked out by the actor himself or between actor and victims. These parties are not likely to work with the fine distinctions that professional lawyers have developed.

One distinction made by Lon Fuller[17] is between a morality of duty on the one hand, specifying the minimum requirements of conduct every citizen must meet and where the appropriate consequence for not meeting these standards is punishment. This is what we traditionally see as the role of law. On the other hand, there is also a morality of aspiration, which specifies how people should act in areas of freedom or autonomy. In the area of creative activity, the appropriate sanction is reward for success, not punishment for failure. Obviously, one must say in areas of legal freedom that one cannot be punished for how one exercises that freedom; otherwise it is not freedom. But the activity of human beings in this area of liberty is not one where society or people are indifferent. One can exercise one's liberties in ways that are creative, valuable, and generous. One can also exercise those liberties in ways that are mean-spirited, greedy, egotistical, and damaging to others. Should not one of the major aims of an ethical system be to operate on how these choices are made?

Another significant distinction is that there is a process inside law by which the validity of the excuse can be determined objectively. This is the trial in which a judge and/or jury will hear the reason given by the actor for not complying with the law and will decide whether it is a justification. The institutions of trial by judge and jury developed over centuries is a satisfactory device to answer such questions. There is a legal specialist, a judge, who controls the legal questions and who has much experience with the resolution of such disputes. The jury is a representative group from the community without special training who brings a fresh viewpoint to a dispute and an understanding of the way ordinary people think and act. Jurors are supposed to resolve all disputed questions of fact. They must reach a majority decision from a number of different points of view. In effect they ask themselves what they would have done in the same situation. If the majority of them would have acted as the defendant, they will probably find the action to be legal and not improper. If the action is out of the ordinary and atypical, they will usually resolve it as having been improper. This compromise between the empathy of ordinary people as jurors evaluating the action and the control of a legally trained and experienced judge tends to produce a substantial number of just decisions.

No such satisfactory procedure for answering disputed questions exists in ethical systems.

NOTES

1. For a fuller discussion of the complexities of causation and how it relates to issues of duty and of damages or sanction, see Banks McDowell, "Foreseeability in Contract and Tort: The Problems of Responsibility and Remoteness," 36 CASE WESTERN RESERVE LAW REV. 286 (1985), and Banks McDowell, "Causation in Contracts and Insurance," 20 CONNECTICUT LAW REV. 569 (1988).

2. The two casebooks I most favored when teaching contracts, Lon Fuller and Melvin Eisenberg, BASIC CONTRACT LAW (St. Paul, Minn.: West Publishing Co., 1972), and Robert W. Hamilton, Alan Scott Rau and Russell J. Weintraub, CASES AND MATERIALS ON CONTRACTS, 2d ed. (St. Paul, Minn.: West Publishing Co., 1992), as well as the much-used John P. Dawson, William Burnett Harvey, and Stanley D. Henderson, CASES AND COMMENT ON CONTRACTS, 5th ed. (Brooklyn: The Foundation Press, 1987), begin with remedies and then consider substantive questions like offer and acceptance, consideration, conditions, and so on. It was thought these could be better understood if one knew what the

likely consequences of each would be. Most students and many contracts scholars find this perverse, but in my view it really reflects the common-law lawyer's attitudes.

3. J. L. Austin, "A Plea for Excuses," PHILOSOPHICAL PAPERS, 3d ed. (Oxford: Oxford University Press, 1979), p. 185.

4. Restatement, Second, Torts (St. Paul, Minn.: American Law Institute, 1965), § 8.

5. William L. Prosser, HANDBOOK OF THE LAW OF TORTS, 4th ed. (St. Paul, Minn.: West Publishing Co., 1971), pp.140–141.

6. BLACK'S LAW DICTIONARY (St. Paul, Minn.: West Publishing Co., 1990), p. 15.

7. There has been an incredible amount of litigation over the meaning and application of such phrases, which Justice Cardozo described as plunging "this branch of the law into a Serbonian bog" (Landress v. Phoenix Ins. Co., 291 U.S. 499 [1933]). There is a good extended discussion of these cases and the problems of interpretation in Robert Keeton and Alan Widiss, INSURANCE LAW, 2d ed. (St. Paul, Minn.: West Publishing Co., 1988), § 5.4.

8. I have argued elsewhere that this element of causation is also a requirement of contracts, although it is seldom overtly discussed. See Banks McDowell, "Causation in Contracts and Insurance," 20 CONNECTICUT LAW REVIEW 569 (1988).

9. American Law Institute, MODEL PENAL CODE, § 204. There is a very interesting discussion of the problems of mistake as a defense in George P. Fletcher, RETHINKING CRIMINAL LAW (Boston: Little, Brown, 1978), Chapter 9.

10. 66 Mich. 568, 33 N.W. 919 (1887).

11. This is a common problem in construction contracts, where a subcontractor makes a bid in which the price has been miscalculated. If the quoted price is so out of line with other subcontractors' bids that it is clear a mistake was made, the general contractor cannot accept it and create a contract. See discussion in Arthur Corbin, CORBIN ON CONTRACTS (St. Paul, Minn.: West Publishing Co., 1960), § 609, and cases cited therein.

12. One context where there has been significant litigation is caused by the so-called "spring-gun" device. When the owner is away, a gun is set to fire at a particular spot, such as a door whenever it is entered. The problem is that innocent people are also at risk. Obviously, the attitude of the court about its legitimacy may be influenced by whether the victim was a burglar or was innocent. See the discussion in Rollin M. Perkins, CRIMINAL LAW (Brooklyn: The Foundation Press, 1957), pp. 920–921.

13. The law tries to influence this choice indirectly in matters of economic assistance by giving tax breaks to those who engage in charitable giving. A social incentive is the medal or public recognition given to someone who acts altruistically by saving another's life or acting with unusual charity.

14. An unresolved problem today is the duty of an adult child to an aged and ill parent. The law has been reluctant to impose a duty of care, while ethics, at least as a matter of contemporary culture, seems to have followed suit by weakening this obligation substantially, but not totally. The curious cultural resolution is that, as this personal obligation of adult children toward elderly parents has weakened, society as a whole has taken on the obligation to care for the elderly through Social

Security and Medicare. This resolution and its cost have become a matter of fierce public and political debate at the moment. Under what circumstances should we transfer what has in the past been individual ethical or legal duties to the state or society?

15. See Banks McDowell, "The Misrepresentation Defense in Insurance: A Problem for Contract Theory," 16 CONNECTICUT LAW REVIEW 513 (1984), for a fuller discussion of fraud as a defense to contractual actions.

16. Lon Fuller used this dilemma as the basis for the creation of his well-known hypothetical teaching case, "The Case of the Speluncean Explorers." See Lon L. Fuller, THE PROBLEMS OF JURISPRUDENCE, temporary edition (Brooklyn: The Foundation Press, 1949), p. 2.

17. Lon L. Fuller, THE MORALITY OF THE LAW (New Haven: Yale University Press, 1964), Chapter 1.

6

The Fallibility of Human Beings

An additional excuse used by professionals who view themselves as decent people is that we are all fallible and that a certain level of ethical wrongdoing is unavoidable. This excuse will most often be raised against claims that the professional performed incompetently, exercised bad judgment, or overlooked something she should have foreseen, such as a doctor making a wrong diagnosis, a lawyer falsely predicting the outcome of a case, a financial advisor making an error in judging how the market will perform, and so on. Not only must there be an error in performance or judgment, but it must cause harm; otherwise, the client will not complain and there is no need for an excuse.

Such a situation often produces different evaluations from the perspective of the professional and that of the dissatisfied client. Although the professional will view the error as a good-faith mistake, the client will consider it as carelessness or incompetence. Can one resolve this disagreement inside the realm of ethics? One possible explanation why so many such disputes end up in court is the law does furnish a mechanism by which there can be a binding resolution.

The ideal resolution, as in most human conflicts, would be reached by mutual agreement. Frank discussion and compromise is not always possible, however, particularly in cases of substantial injury. There is a natural tendency for the professional, who may feel some degree of guilt, to avoid talking about the problem. Ideally, there should be a full discussion with the client about the reasons for the choices made and an attempt to meet the client's dissatisfaction. If the dispute or the differing perceptions remain, some more efficient procedure for resolution needs to be developed, perhaps a third-party mediator, a professional ombudsman made available by the professional organizations, or some other less costly and adversarial procedure than legal remedies provide.

For some decades, this has been a difficult issue for the medical profession, fueled in part by the popular belief that doctors are scientists and medical science can give reliable diagnoses and successful therapy for illness. As Samuel Gorovitz has written:

> Patients and the public have to learn to recognize, accept, and respond reasonably to the necessary fallibility of the individual physician. The physician-patient relationship is one in which mistakes necessarily will be made, sometimes culpably, sometimes because of the state of development of medical science, but sometimes, ineliminably, because of the inherent limitations on the predictive powers of an enterprise concerned essentially with the flourishing of particular, complex, fragile individuals.[1]

Defendants in malpractice suits routinely describe their misconduct as only a minor error and blame greedy lawyers and ungrateful clients for suing. The error is not seen as something the professional is really responsible for, so he does not feel it is necessary to alter conduct, except defensively to be prepared for the next lawsuit.

It may be a truism that we are all fallible, but an important one to remember because most of us continue to be trapped to some degree by the illusion of perfectibility.[2] We increasingly understand in the everyday world that the people we deal with, our neighbors, our colleagues, and our relatives, are human and cannot always be ethical in their choices and flawless in their performance. For those of us who are conscientious and ethical, whether we on occasion do damage through good-faith errors or not is much a matter of luck or good fortune.[3] We necessarily have a certain tolerance for human weakness as long as it does not happen too often or produce too much damage. Should we extend that same tolerance to professionals?

The claim of professionals to an allowance for mistakes presents a different and more subtle problem. They create a higher set of expectations about their performance. The unrealistic expectation that professionals should be infallible has been in part the product of professionalism and the competition of professionals in a market economy. One way of analyzing the status of being a professional is that each profession and individual practitioner claims a monopoly of expertise in a particular field, a jealously guarded monopoly. Two well-known examples have been the battle of medical doctors against chiropractors and lawyers against accountants in the field of tax law. In these battles over contested "turf," the professional claims he is the only one who can understand and solve the client's problems. This sets up high expectations of performance by the client. Not only does the profession create a protected territory, but it feels driven by market forces to increase the demand for professional services. Potential clients must be persuaded they need more legal services, more medical care, better record keeping by accountants, and so on. Within each profession, there is competition by individuals or professional groups to attract clients away from other professionals. A central part of this competitive marketing strategy is to make strong claims about the necessity of the services and the superiority of the particular professional. The defense against exaggerated claims by service providers is supposed to be an informed consumer who can make wise choices among suppliers. The more sophisticated consumers might be skeptical about excessive claims of competence, but generally it is an area where even sophisticated clients have little understanding; otherwise there is often little need to hire the professional.

An almost natural consequence of this competitive situation is for professionals to make the strongest possible claims of competence, which create high expectations, which will sometimes be disappointed. One claim that will be made at least tacitly, in addition to technical expertise, is about the character issue of professionalism. "You can trust me." "You can feel sure that your confidences are safe." "You will get the highest level of excellence from my services." These excessive levels of expectation will sometimes produce disappointment and the feeling that the professional has fallen below tolerable levels of satisfactory performance.

One obvious way to minimize the necessity for this excuse is to lower clients' expectations of what professionals can do. This ought to be done at the beginning of the relationship before any risky performance is begun. This more modest set of claims to competence also involves abandoning a highly competitive marketing strategy that has produced increased financial success for many individual professionals.

There is another expectation game I have seen professionals play when they are not engaged in direct competition with other professionals for a particular client. That is to present unreasonably low predictions about probabilities of success, so they appear to have been exceptionally brilliant in achieving results that, unknown to the client, were to be expected.

Clearly the ethical duty in both situations is to honestly assess the probabilities of success at the point of hiring so the client has the best available information to make choices about whether to hire this particular professional and whether to proceed with a particular course of action.

If the client's high expectations are disappointed, he feels that a promise has been breached, almost as if he has been defrauded. The stronger this feeling of having been tricked, the less likely the excuse that it was just a good-faith mistake will be acceptable.

DESCRIPTION AND/OR EXCUSE

Should we regard the concept of human fallibility as a description of personality or an ethical excuse? If it is an excuse, some norm must have been violated. A norm or ideal, by definition, must be more than descriptive of behavior. Otherwise, the norm would seldom, if ever, be breached and there would be little need for excuses. On the other hand, if the gap between ideal and conduct is too broad and deep, there will be serious problems of compliance. Then excuses will regularly be offered and routinely accepted.

What type of description one adopts of the human personality and its potentiality is a critical one for ethical theory and for practical ethics? One possible view is that human beings are rational, intelligent, capable of exercising will power, and can control themselves and their environment. Another is that human beings are irrational, often uninformed or unaware, easily manipulated, and subject to internal or external pressures that give them little control over themselves or their environment. My personal view is that while both descriptions are potentially accurate, the evidence available today supports the latter more than the former. This perception would place greater emphasis on the necessity for developing guiding and controlling systems, of which ethics is clearly an important, but not sufficient one.

Which of these competing views are selected as the basis for understanding human actors is partly a question of perception, that is, of how accurately and without illusions we see ourselves and other people, and partly a matter of finding what we want to see and what our values make us pick out of a complex set of people and interrelationships. Much social science analysis and research is an attempt to answer these questions empirically. A serious error we must all guard against is taking our perception of what ought to be as descriptive of the reality of what is.

Why this choice of categorization is difficult is that we are asking two questions or thinking on two different levels, and we often blend the two. What *ought* the person to be or do? And what *is* he as a person? On the level of ethics, we expect a human being to strive for those qualities that much ethical analysis and norms are built on, that is, rationality, intelligence, decency, and strong self-control. While those are desirable goals or ideals, they are hardly descriptive statements and for many people, including professionals, far from being realized, or easily realizable. This gives rise to the excuse that is the subject of this chapter.

When conduct is viewed as normal or average or acceptable, there is little need for excuses. It is only the abnormal that must be excused and requires change in behavior. This is not to say that normal or average conduct is immune from criticism. And one important role of morals or ethics is to criticize the accepted practices and actions, to see if they need changing.

Is it abnormal for decent and careful people to occasionally make mistakes or be careless? The question answers itself. All of us from the most decent and careful to the meanest and most thoughtless make mistakes.

Professional ethics, which should be guidelines for people struggling with complex and difficult problems, must be practical. A practical ethics must tolerate some mistakes and condemn others. The important problem is to decide what should be tolerated and what condemned.

THE ZONE FOR TOLERANCE

If we accept that, on the continuum of human acts ranging from the intentionally unethical to the unquestionably ethical, there needs to be an area where we will be tolerant of human error, how should we demarcate that zone?

That middle zone in which mistakes will occur is generally characterized by terms like carelessness, thoughtlessness, imprudence. Carelessness, a middle position between intentional injury and accidental happenings, has become for lawyers, who label it negligence, the most important theory of civil liability in tort law. That portion of acts, even by prudent and competent professionals, that could potentially fall into this zone of carelessness where mistakes occur is substantial. One could not contend that ethics, or the law, should be indifferent about all acts within that area. In this large zone of careless activity, we need to refine those occurrences into groups of those we condemn, those we tolerate, and those we find unexceptional. I suggest three factors that would help in drawing those distinctions: (a) intent or motive, (b) seriousness of injury caused, and (c) amount of experience of the actor.

As long as the professional acts in good faith, that is, without the intent to harm and out of good motives, should that excuse unethical conduct? We saw in the last chapter that intent is often an element in legal responsibility. Should it be any different in ethics?

In an interesting discussion, J. L. Austin suggests that doing something intentionally is an aggravating factor, which makes the wrongdoing more serious and more blameworthy,[4] but he does not suggest lack of intentionality avoids wrongdoing or blame altogether.

What level of care removes those actions that produce harm to others from the realm of unethical and should that be defined differently than the line drawn by lawyers between negligence and acting with due care? For a long time, the common law asked jurors to distinguish slight negligence, ordinary negligence, and gross negligence. There were certain types of liability for which the plaintiff had to establish gross or extreme negligence. Other times ordinary negligence would suffice. In most cases slight negligence would not create legal liability. These distinctions were largely abandoned in tort law because of the administrative difficulties of defining the standards that separated the three classes and the problems jurors had in applying those standards. While law has to worry about the problems of clearly defined standards and reliable proof, ethics is freer to work without such administrative worries. If these distinctions of great, ordinary, and slight carelessness can be applied, it is possible to graduate the seriousness of those mistakes that might be labeled as unethical acts. Normally, we are careful enough, particularly in dangerous situations, to act in ways that would not be designated grossly negligent or extremely careless. We are frequently guilty of slight negligence, carelessness, or inadvertence, and often enough guilty of such ordinary negligence as to keep the lawyers at the tort bar busy. As far as intention is concerned, those activities that are in genuine good faith or involve only slight carelessness or negligence could be one defining factor in our zone of tolerance.

In deciding whether the action should be treated as intentional, careless, or in sufficient good faith, one factor might be the seriousness of harm that could be foreseen as likely to happen. Trivial matters are less likely to be given serious attention. Another defining factor for intentionality would be rareness of the occurrence. It is possible to argue that a very unusual or aberrational violation of an ethical norm could not have been foreseen as probable, was not likely to be intended, and thus should not be grounds for blaming the actor or labeling her an unethical person. Here, we are trying to indicate what factors go into deciding when we can foresee the necessity to act with care.

The second element in defining our zone of tolerance is the amount of harm caused by the wrongdoing. While one might contend that the degree of injury is not relevant to the question of wrongdoing, in the practical world it makes an enormous difference. The degree of care and attention a person devotes to complying with norms or guidelines does turn on the probability of doing serious injury. One example comes from G. L. Warnock: "If I knock over the pepper-pot inadvertence will get me off the hook, but not if I knock over your Sevres vase."[5] A more common example is the everyday experience of driving a car. A person is more likely to drive with great care on a crowded street where any variation from the expected pattern will cause an accident than when she is on an empty highway. What controls her degree of care is the anticipation of the likelihood of an accident happening and, if it does happen, the probability that injuries to herself, her automobile, or other persons will occur and/or be serious. Should not that kind of analysis enter into assessing ethical responsibility for her actions?

Should it be the actual seriousness of the injury or the foreseeability of the likelihood that serious injury will occur that would control our judgment? One must distinguish between the action itself and its consequences. Injury is a consequence and whether it will occur and how serious it will be is often outside the foreseeability and the control of the actor. On the other hand, the victim, often the client, has to deal with the fact of injury and is not greatly interested in whether the professional could or should have foreseen it prior to acting.

A third factor in defining the zone is the experience and competence of the actor. In any area of human activity, we understand that the beginner, apprentice, or neophyte will more likely make mistakes, so the zone of tolerance for mistakes will be much greater than that which would be allowed for an experienced performer.

In most professional institutions, whether we are talking about law firms, medical hospitals, accounting firms, or any other organization where professional apprentices are trained, the beginner will be monitored and watched carefully so his mistakes will not do serious damage. As the monitoring decreases with time and the professional is allowed more autonomy in the practice of the profession, the zone of tolerance for mistakes shrinks.

In defining the zone of tolerance, we are using three factors, which must interact in some form of balance. There will be cases where the most extreme good faith, the best of intentions, and the inexperience of the actor will not excuse actions that have produced very serious injury. We must bear the consequences of taking risky action where the result, however unforeseeable, was very damaging to others. There would also be cases where the carelessness is so extreme or the intention so malevolent that the actor is responsible for very slight damage done. Then there is the question of the amount of experience and competence the performer has. Thus, our zone of tolerance is defined by a substantial degree of good faith (or only minor negligence), by lack of serious harm arising from the action, and the degree of experience and competence that should control whether mistakes are frequent or relatively rare.

Obviously the downside of accepting this excuse in the case of good-faith mistakes or errors in judgment is that unscrupulous, incompetent, and unethical professionals can make the claim and it may be difficult to decide which type of professional and what type of ethical or professional error we are dealing with. Still, these are problems in any practical system of normative judgments that must be applied to human activity. One always has cases on the periphery or borderline about which difficult decisions must be made. Since borderline problems can never be eliminated, we need to accept that fact and deal with it clearly and openly.

Much ethical discussion still assumes that ethical human beings should not have such lapses. This is not a weak excuse, however, because we all, however competent and decent, cannot go through a professional life without some misjudgments or ethical lapses.[6] While we might expect well-made machines to perform flawlessly, we know that is impossible for humans. A practical ethics for professionals cannot insist on perfect performance always. The degree of mistakes made in good faith that are acceptable has been an underdeveloped issue in professional ethics and that should be clarified so the actor or others can still label himself or herself as an ethical being.

It should be clear that what we are defining here is the area in which the excuse will or should be persuasive. There will be mistakes for which the professional must take full ethical responsibility. There will also be mistakes that could not have been normally avoidable and for which no serious ethical blame should attach. The problem is defining the two categories and deciding into which one a particular human case of mistaken error belongs.

ANALYSIS OF THE GOOD-FAITH-MISTAKE PROBLEM

Throughout this chapter, I have used the word "tolerance" in connection with "mistakes." Both terms are ambiguous and can create problems in clear thinking. What counts as a "mistake?" What are the connotations of "tolerance" in relationship to blame and from whom must it come?

When we describe an outcome as a mistake, we mean that it was unexpected and unwanted. Further, it was an outcome that could have been prevented by a different course of action. It lies between a true accident and prudent and careful performance by the professional. Mistakes are unavoidable in professional practice. Often what the professional is selling is judgment about a complex situation where the diagnosis or recommendation can be selected out of a series of possibilities, all with varying degrees of probability about being correct. Sometimes the judgment, given in good faith and one that other competent professionals would have given in the same situation, produces an unwanted outcome. The result may be substantial injury to the client, who will often feel the judgment was incompetent or unethical. One of the hardest problems in judging whether a human actor was wrong in making judgments is avoiding hindsight evaluation. In fairness, one should place oneself in the same state of knowledge the actor had when deciding when and how to act. That is a particularly difficult perspective for the client to take both because of lack of technical knowledge and because of self-interest. If the professional person will regularly be judged as acting illegally or unethically for good-faith errors in judgment or diagnosis, that will inevitably lead to more cautious practice and an unwillingness to engage in experimental procedures or to take risks.

In general, tolerance comes not from the actor, but from others. While it is possible to say I tolerate actions I have taken myself, that is an awkward and atypical usage. When I say I tolerate some action of another person or even of myself, the word signifies that it is not an activity I approve of. It is not okay to make mistakes. That activity is not to be accepted or encouraged. At the same time, it is not to be totally condemned or prohibited. Trial and error is a major way we learn. One should learn from one's mistakes and over time reduce the number made. One distinguishing characteristic between neophytes and the competent and experienced professional is that while the competent professional still make mistakes, they will be fewer and usually less damaging.

If we accept that there should be some tolerance for decent people who aberrationally make mistakes or act in an unethical way, we can deal with that at three points: (1) in the formulation of the ethical norm itself, (2) in accepting this as an excuse that avoids or minimizes responsibility, or (3) in the consequences of the judgment, that is, the amount of blame and the seriousness of any sanctions placed against the actor. Which of these three options is the point at which we do or ought to resolve the issue of good-faith mistakes?

In considering whether one should deal with this problem at the normative stage, we need first to examine exactly how we would formulate the standard that a mistake could be said to violate. Is it that one should never make mistakes? Is it that one should be careful and prudent in one's actions? Is it that one should try to avoid making mistakes, but that there is an exception for the good-faith mistake, which does not cause much damage?

A major reason for adopting the first form of the norm that does not allow for aberrations even in good faith is a perfectionist view of human beings; that is, if a person cannot be perfect, he or she should always strive toward perfection, which in turn will lead to growth and personal improvement. That approach, however, leads to bad descriptive statements about ourselves and others when we are discussing our actions and our moralities, as well as to unrealistic expectations that we will regularly fail to fulfill, leading to self-doubts and disgust.

The second formulation recognizes that one can make mistakes and does not set such a hopelessly high standard of expectation. It requires only that one act with normal care and prudence. It is not easy to establish acceptable standards as to what kinds of deviation from perfect conduct are acceptable, both in percentages of occurrence and in seriousness. We can start from the expectation that humans are or can be perfect and think of any conduct that does not meet that standard as aberrational and subject to blame. On the other hand, we could think of conduct that includes some level of good-faith carelessness as normal and then consider only deviations below that standard as worthy of ethical condemnation. The second approach gives less clear guidelines and calls for much better descriptive knowledge about actual conduct than we currently tend to gather and use. From an ethical perspective, it would leave more tolerable levels of blame and guilt for decent people.

The third formulation, which creates an exception, is in essence selecting the stage of sanction or reaction as the point of dealing with this issue. This tolerance for human fallibility could be built into the application of the norm, the third option, based on the seriousness of the ethical violation and its consequences, analogous to the choice judges have among imposing heavy sentences or light sentences, placing an offender on probation, or merely admonishing the offender. This analysis would suggest that the claim that the action was a good-faith error, or a mistake, is a mitigating, not an avoidance, excuse.

The consequence of not dealing with this at the norm stage is that a decent, good-faith professional is then faced with the internal or external judgment that his or her act was unethical, but that it was excused because of the rare nature of the occurrence, that it was not serious, or some other such reason. Decent people are those most likely to feel the blame for unethical conduct as shameful and thus to have the heaviest degree of guilt. For those of us who view ourselves as ethical, the way this issue is analyzed and labeled matters. Many of us carry around with us unusually heavy loads of guilt, sometimes justified, but often not necessary. A practical ethic that hopes to have real effect on people's action should use its major weapon, guilt, sparingly so that it will have maximum effect in those situations where it is most likely to be needed.

There seems no easy way to resolve the dilemma posed by the good-faith mistake. We want the ethical expectations of ourselves and others to be demanding in order that we continue to improve. At that level, we need an aspirational ethics that pulls us always toward being better professionals and better people. On the other hand, there is the high personal cost and psychological damage done when the ethical person does not attain those levels or occasionally falls below the line. How can we mix tolerance for ourselves and others because we are fallible human beings with the expectation that we must seriously strive always to be better? That may be the most difficult issue faced by a practical system of ethics and the reason to have an ethical, rather than a legal, system govern the conduct of decent people who try to do well, but on occasion fail. The irony is that the law, which is supposed to be more rigid and punitive, is actually much more tolerant of human frailty than ethics.

THE CONSEQUENCES OF GOOD-FAITH MISTAKES

The process of deciding whether a professional or someone else should be ethically responsible for a mistake is complex and unclear. Is being "responsible" merely an evaluative judgment or is it a matter of the sanctions that follow? Is it a matter of blame from clients or victims? Is it a question of whether the actor feels guilt? The consequence of "tolerating" a good-faith mistake means that some degree of blame is attached.

In the case of a good-faith mistake that might have been avoidable with better foresight and heightened levels of care, we do not want to relieve the actor of all blame. On the other hand, we do not want to censure him as severely as we would have had he acted intentionally or with great want of care. How does one find the right amount of blame to accompany the zone of tolerance we talked about above?

We are used in law and to a great extent in ethics to judge acts and not actors; that is to say, we concentrate on the individual act and do not focus on the character of the actor. There is a general requirement, at least in a formal sense, that one be a person of good moral character in order to be licensed and to continue as a member of the profession.[7] This may be a holdover from an earlier time when professionals were parts of smaller communities and were judged as much on character as on technical expertise. If character is the important question, can we then infer back from the act, often a single one, the existence of an unethical, weak, or bad character? Is it not more accurate to say that if we blame someone for committing a good-faith mistake, we are blaming the act, but not the person? The person is ethical, the act not. If we blame someone for an intentional act or grossly careless action, we are inclined to blame the person as well as the act.

We all recognize the difference between a good or decent person who will occasionally and untypically act in an unethical way that damages others, and one who has a disposition or propensity to act unethically. The latter is a ground for denying the person a license to practice as a professional. The aberrational unethical act is not one that should lead to that sort of total condemnation. The occasional unethical act of a moral and decent human would usually be in the range of a careless, inattentive, or unusual act, rather than an intentional and regular practice. For such occasional acts, it is not necessary to blame the actor, but merely the act. People of decent character will try to minimize or eliminate as far as humanly possible such activities. The blame of others or of her own conscience leads to minimizing the careless activity of a decent person, so the blame should be directed to condemning the individual act, not the character of the actor.

If it is necessary or desirable for some level of tolerance to be developed for good-faith aberrations of decent people, it is not the tolerance of the objective observer or a tolerance of a theoretical system of ethics, but a tolerance from the victim that is most important. In all human interactions, a give-and-take or a reciprocal attitude is essential. The person injured is the one most entitled to complain about unethical actions and also the one who must have some level of tolerance or understanding for the human frailties of people with whom he is doing business, including professionals. It is only in the dialogue in which excuses play the dominant role that a workable balance between tolerance of mistakes by victims and high expectations of professional performance can be worked out in particular contexts.

There is one final problem to be dealt with. If we have a situation where the professional has performed in a way that does not satisfy the client, there is a loss to the client, and the excuse that it was a good-faith mistake is acceptable to the client or a third-party observer, is there an ethical duty on the professional practitioner or the profession as a whole to ameliorate or cover the loss?

This is an ideal place to use the device of insurance. In dealing with professionals, unfortunately, the type of insurance currently used is liability insurance and in order for that to be available, the professional has had to incur legal liability, which is to say the courts have found or would be likely to find that this was a case of malpractice. This is inconsistent with saying that it was a good-faith mistake. The courts, desiring to compensate the victim for professional errors produced by a good-faith mistake, must label it as serious wrongdoing in order to unlock the insurance proceeds. Perhaps a better analog that could be used here to develop protection for good-faith mistakes would be the concept of products liability insurance developed when it was not possible or proper to find the manufacturer or retailer of a defective product at fault. This is a kind of insurance scheme developed to spread the loss across all consumers by charging each a small increase in the price to create an insurance fund that would be used to compensate those who actually were injured. This has not raised serious practical or cost problems in manufacturers' liability because the incidence of serious injury from a defective product is sufficiently low in comparison to the number of products sold that the cost to each consumer is not large. The mistakes professionals make that they would like to have labeled good-faith mistakes are proportionately larger. We can see this in the cost of malpractice insurance among some specialties, such as obstetrics or neurosurgery where unsatisfactory performance is sufficiently frequent and expensive that the "insurance" cost which must be passed on to consumers or to health insurers is very great indeed.

NOTES

1. Samuel Gorovitz, DOCTORS' DILEMMAS: MORAL CONFLICT AND MEDICAL CARE (New York: MacMillan, 1982), pp. 29–30.

2. A penetrating analysis of the demand for and difficulties inherent in a quest for perfection is found in Ernest Becker, THE DENIAL OF DEATH (New York: Free Press, 1973), particularly pp. 184–186.

3. There is a good discussion of how the element of luck relates to the well-intentioned, but mistaken actions of decent people in Joel Feinberg, DOING AND DESERVING (Princeton: University of Princeton Press, 1970), pp. 191–192.

4. J. L. Austin, "Three Ways of Spilling Ink," PHILOSOPHICAL PAPERS, 3d ed. (Oxford: Oxford University Press, 1979), p. 273.

5. G. L. Warnock, J. L. AUSTIN (London and New York: Routledge, 1991), p. 79.

6. See Bernd Guggenberger, DAS MENSCHENRECHT AUF IRRTUM (Munich and Vienna: Carl Hanser Verlag, 1987). Guggenberger, a well-known German social theorist, argues that the modern complex world makes human error much more devastating and yet human error is a necessary and valuable happening, since it is only through trial and error that we make progress. He argues we must develop a mistake-friendly environment in which errors are expected and do not do irreparable damage.

7. See Deborah Rhode, "Moral Character as a Professional Credential, 94 YALE LAW JOURNAL 491 (1985) and Banks McDowell, "The Usefulness of 'Good Moral Character'," WASHBURN LAW JOURNAL 323 (1994).

7

The Informal Moral Codes

Most of the discussion and teaching of professional ethics accepts the formal professional codes as the grounding and the authoritative promulgation of ethical norms for the profession. The formal professional codes do have certain important functions. Their preamble, hortatory language, and general principles set up the profession's high aspirations or goals, although at a sufficiently abstract level that they seldom provide practitioners with adequate practical guidelines. The formal codes set outer limits on the range of acceptable conduct. Finally, they are public-relations documents, which tell the public in what ways a member of the particular profession differs or is supposed to differ from ordinary service providers.

In professional schools, students master the subject matter of the formal code sufficiently well to pass an examination and then tend to forget its details as they do much of the other formal knowledge they have learned and then have little direct use for. The code will usually be revisited only during public pronouncements about the honor of being a professional or when a professional is accused of having acted unethically. Although it may be used to establish unethical conduct, it is used more often to show that in fact the questionable conduct was in compliance with the code, that is, as an excuse.

Behind or beside the formal code is an informal moral code for professional activity.[1] Such informal codes also exist for the society as a whole and affect professionals as well. We are all responsible to layers of morality: first, the formal ethical principles one learns from religious, cultural, and formal education; second, an informal moral code learned from watching how people act and what peers and friends expect; third, the formal specialized professional code; and, finally, an informal code among professionals, learned in much the same way as the informal social code. While these codes contain many of the same principles, they vary in the level of abstractness, the degree of universality, the weight of particular precepts, and the adaptation of general principles to the needs of smaller identifiable communities. It would be a miracle if these various moralities did not occasionally conflict.

Before one can understand the dissonances between the formal moral codes, whether professional or social, and the informal moral codes, as well as the dissonances between those two codes and actual behavior, it is important to get a good picture of what informal moral codes consist of. Informal moral codes control behavior more than formal codes. They are closer to the real morality of an actor and of people.

Informal codes are more flexible and often better adapted to particular situations. There is, of course, less universality in informal moralities than formal ones.[2] They belong to smaller communities and frequently belong to communities that are defined on other than geographical lines, such as generational, religious, ethnic background, profession or trade, and so on. Because informal codes are seldom discussed publicly, and not frozen into a fixed formulation, one is never exactly sure what the social consensus is. That is a quality shared with excuses. Both are important parts of our world, but remain only semiconscious or rather a part of the background, so we are never sure what the precise contents of either the informal social morality or of acceptable excuses are. The fact that they are only semiconscious does not mean they do not exist or do not exercise a powerful force upon us.

How does one learn informal moral codes? People are always making choices, always acting. From among these actions and choices, which ones are ethical? Here, the adjective "ethical" is not used to signify that the particular choice was proper. Rather it indicates the choice falls into the realm of ethics. If ethical choices are those that produce good or bad results, we constantly learn from the reaction of others. When we make a choice that, is criticized by a parent, sibling, teacher, friend, or employer, we often give an excuse or an explanation which, if not accepted, means that significant others find we did not follow the accepted moral code of conduct. We learn partly by observing others and partly from adverse reactions to the way we have acted. This is how children learn what is not done or is not acceptable. It is also how neophyte professionals learn. They watch how other professionals act and they, as beginners, make mistakes and are criticized. A portion of the professional neophyte's mistakes is technical; many are bad choices in ethical dilemmas. This is not formal, but practical education. It is not only a matter of learning to apply principles, but also of learning and applying certain kinds of precepts that may differ from formal ones.

To understand a culture, you must know its language. This applies equally to subcultures, like a profession. You must also know the informal morality of that culture. Just as language changes and has regional and local patterns, so does any informal morality. If one uses language as a metaphor, formal moral codes are like the rules of grammar, spelling, and syntax that language scholars and teachers have polished over centuries and try to compel speakers to use. Informal moral codes are like ordinary language and slang, changing over time and varying from region to region. To have a complete picture of a language, one must know both the ideal language and ordinary usage. To have a complete picture of a culture's morality, one must know both the formal and informal codes.

The moral systems that professionals respond to may be categorized or analyzed in a variety of ways. Another insightful distinction among such moralities was made by Jane Jacobs in *Systems Of Survival*,[3] where she describes a commercial moral syndrome, that is, a morality for people engaged in commerce, and a guardian moral syndrome, a morality for people in government and the military. They contain many opposite principles. An important example is the principle that people in commerce are expected to engage in trade, while people in government are expected to avoid trade and be loyal to the institution they belong to.[4] These competing moralities can pose problems for professionals, particularly lawyers. Lawyers in private practice belong to the commercial moral syndrome; judges and lawyers in governmental service to the guardian syndrome. It is clearly immoral for lawyers in the governmental realm to trade or sell their services. That constitutes bribery. The problem is lawyers are trained to work in both realms indifferently. Many lawyers move back and forth between the two realms in their careers. If they bring the morality from one arena into the other, they are likely to be perceived as performing unethically.

One character in Jane Jacob's fictional group when discussing the role of the governmental professionals suggests that they are bound strongly by tradition and says: "Tradition helps serve as a substitute for conscience in guardian work. That may be tradition's most important moral meaning. Normally, it sets limits to what's done."[5] Obviously, judges are strongly bound by tradition. Although people in private commercial activity tend to disparage tradition as limiting and stultifying, it does have an important moral role to play, particularly for those who exercise the power of the state.

Excuses may point to two quite different matters in relationship to informal moralities. One is an attempt to explain and justify an action by a claim that the actor was complying with the informal code, rather than the formal one. Another is to highlight a conflict between formal and informal codes. As we shall see later, excuses may also point out inconsistencies and conflicts in the informal code.

My discussion in this chapter mixes both the general informal social morality that controls everybody in the society and the informal professional moral code. They are not clearly separated in our thinking. Human actors as organic beings are influenced by both informal systems in all their activities, whether professional or not.

When we discuss in the next chapter whether ethical standards ought to be reformulated, among the questions to be considered are: (1) should we bring the formal ethical code more in consonance with the informal moral codes, (2) should we try to influence the informal codes to bring them in line with the less flexible principles of the formal code, or (3) do both formal and informal codes need to be reworked to give better guidelines for the ethical problems faced by professionals in contemporary practice? Those questions cannot be addressed until we have a clearer picture of what the informal moral codes provide.

Among the precepts belonging to the informal moral code most of us are raised in and obey to some extent are the following, using as far as possible their formulation in ordinary language. They are listed roughly in the order both of their certainty and of their strength. While I am fairly certain these are informal moral rules in my society and in my profession, I am less sure whether the listing is in the order of their strength. The listing is not meant to be exhaustive, but illustrative to show the differences between formal and informal moral codes.

1. *"Be true to your own kind."* This precept represents a powerful sense of loyalty to small groups, such as family, friends, community, and ethnic groups. Loyalty is a major, if not the major, virtue for professionals in relationship both to their clients and to their profession. This precept produces the "we—them" phenomenon where strong loyalty to those close to you carries with it limited loyalty, and sometimes even contempt, for out-groups. In modern complex cultures, the lines of loyalty are less clear than in simpler, homogeneous societies. Today each individual identifies himself as belonging to a number of groups creating conflicts in loyalty. The groups may be defined by kinship, by religion, by age, by geographical location, by occupation, by gender, and so on. For professionals *qua* professionals, loyalty belongs to their clients, their work groups, and the profession itself.

The members of the "we" group enjoy different moral relationships with the actor than do others. Members of the out-groups are not entitled to as much protection or consideration, nor are they considered as trustworthy. At times, they can be exploited or taken advantage of without any feeling of moral blame or remorse.

A corollary, or perhaps the result, of this proposition is that you are taught to be cautious, if not suspicious, of strangers or of those you do not know well. Strangers are different, so they may not have any loyalty to you and may have very different real rules of conduct.

This strong informal principle conflicts with the formal commitment in our society to equality of treatment for everyone regardless of their particular class characteristics, whether those distinctions be based on religion, gender, race, or ethnic origin. Modern egalitarianism blurs lines of loyalty. As a reflection of the formal moral principles of my contemporary culture, I dislike hierarchical organizations, authoritarianism, and parochialism, but those structural attitudes do have the advantage of making clearer to whom loyalties are owed.

For professionals, there is a conflict between formal and informal professional codes on just this point. In fact, this conflict is where I first noticed the distinction between formal and informal codes. As a young and somewhat cynical lawyer, I noticed early in my practice much to my surprise that there was a strong ethical code at work among the lawyers in the medium-sized city where I worked. I could trust without question any promise made to me by another lawyer and could normally expect cooperation even from opposing lawyers on most matters requiring accommodation and understanding. This was a different morality from what I had been taught in my professional ethics course. The formal code stressed strongly loyalty to the client and the client's interests as a central, if not the central, focus of professional ethics. The informal professional code emphasized strong loyalty to the professional group and the interests of other professionals. The formal and informal codes incorporate both loyalties, but give them different strengths or emphases. Many practitioners face situations where the zealous protection of a client's interests does not coincide with the accommodations expected between professionals and therefore tough choices have to be made, usually without guidance or help on the extent to which you follow the formal or the informal code.

2. *"Work hard and get ahead."* One should aspire to material success and power in the group to which one belongs. Is this properly labeled a moral rule? If moral rules lay down guidelines as to how one ought to act, this clearly belongs. In the worldview of our culture, this famous "work ethic" is assumed to be the reason for the success of the "Western world." Those without ambition for material success are criticized as lazy or worthless. There is an imperative to have the means to live a decent life and to have power. Both power and money are often said to be neutral values, neither good nor bad, but rather instrumentalities that take on an ethical character depending on how they are used. The problem is that a deficiency or an excess of either can create its own set of problems. Too little wealth or power makes it impossible for a person to do good or much else in life. An excessive drive to obtain either money or power costs people who get in the way, as well as the actor, a great deal.

A perversion of this moral value is produced by extremely competitive situations, such as professional sports, aggressive capitalist activities, and, in my experience, professional schools. In these contexts, winning or being the very best takes on an obsessive quality. When that is coupled with the excuse that if it is legal, it cannot be unethical, some exceedingly unethical activity may occur.

Ethics not only has a responsibility to define what amount of success is enough, but also the ways in which the struggle for sufficient wealth and power to live a decent life and to be able to do the things that matter to the actor should be constrained so that undue damage is not done to other people.

This informal but powerful moral rule that one should seek material success not only produces large levels of guilt among those of us who do not work as hard as we possibly could, but also contributes to much of today's cynicism. We have been taught to believe that hard work should produce success. There is a widespread feeling today that those who get ahead do so not because of hard work or even of ability, but because of influence, luck, or acting in ways that are unethical. Remember that one of the subexcuses under the heading of irresistible pressure was that my competitors are acting unethically and I must do so in order to keep up with them. Another piece of evidence showing cynicism about this moral rule is the frequent discussion today about the importance of "networking," that is, building a collection of friends or allies who will help you get ahead just because you are their friend or because of their expectation of reciprocal help. Obviously, there is nothing wrong and much to be said for having numerous acquaintances who can help you get ahead in the world, but if that is what produces success rather than hardwork, it undercuts the belief in this moral principle.

3. *"Don't rock the boat."* One should not be a troublemaker, a difficult person for others. Most North Americans feel strong pressure to merge into the group in action, dress, behavior, taste, and culture. This is not a new phenomenon. De Tocqueville already noticed it in the early nineteenth century. Anyone who is demonstrably different and who raises unpleasant matters or causes discomfort is frowned on. In other words, the conformist, the one who believes in and practices social harmony, is preferred.[6] This can produce serious problems for legal practitioners, particularly for young aspirants to the law. Lawyers by historical definition are troublemakers, battlers, aggressive. Many young people who have been socialized not to be troublemakers have difficulty in adjusting to the traditional role of the lawyer as litigator.

This informal guideline conflicts directly with our mythic picture of ourselves as highly individualistic, adventuresome, creative, entrepreneurial people. It also conflicts with the second precept requiring hard work and success. Success causes the person to stand out, to emerge from the crowd. Many young people are torn between adhering to the second or the third of these informal precepts.

4. *"Treat me with respect."* This is usually cast in the form that the speaker demands to be treated with respect by others. It does imply an understanding that reciprocity requires like treatment to others. That this demand to be

treated with respect and dignity is a basic and fundamental informal moral notion is testified to by the fact that even outsider groups in our society, such as convicts in prison or gang members in the inner city, expect it to such a degree that if they feel they are being treated with disrespect, they will respond with extreme violence. One of the constant complaints of people on governmental welfare and the recipients of private charity is that they feel they have lost respect and are treated with "benign" contempt by more privileged members of the society.

5. *"Mind your own business."* This is probably a product of modern urban atomized life. In older smaller communities where people knew each other well, everyone minded everybody else's business to a substantial degree. This urban adage reflects the importance of privacy and a wariness about getting involved with strangers in situations where you know neither the people nor the environment well enough to be sure about the right thing to do. The negative side of this proposition is that people allow much damaging and unethical activity to occur within their knowledge or vicinity without feeling any desire or entitlement to intervene. There is in Jane Jacob's *The Death and Life of Great American Cities* a marvelous description of how important is a willingness to be involved with what occurs on the sidewalks where one lives and works for developing and maintaining vital and safe city neighborhoods.[7]

In connection with professional activity, Samuel Gorovitz makes the point that:

> [T]he business of medicine is essentially the minding of other people's business, albeit in a limited way. So the physician cannot escape moral dilemmas by deciding to mind his own business—medical decision—while leaving to others the responsibility of minding theirs. Medicine is by its nature intrusive in the lives of its consumers; the providers therefore cannot escape the fact that there are ethical dimensions of nearly all they do.[8]

Of course, this point applies not only to doctors, who mind the health business of their patients, but to lawyers, who mind the legal business of their clients, to accountants, who mind the financial business of their customers, and to ministers, who mind the spiritual business of their parishioners. When professionals say they are only performing tasks involving technical expertise and not making value or ethical judgments on behalf of clients, they are consciously or unconsciously masking the degree to which they intermeddle and mind the business of people they serve.

The injunction "mind your own business" can also be used by professionals to avoid many ethical dilemmas and hard value choices by arguing that these are the business of the client, not the professional. They may view themselves as technical specialists for whom these kinds of difficult value questions are out of bounds. They may also pick and choose in what ways they will manage the business or the client by saying that certain matters are questions of professional concern and that any others are not the concern of the professional. As long as the professional is the one making the decision on whether to intervene or not, she is without effective controls. Professional ethics should define better what is the business of each professional and to what extent they are entitled to intervene.

There will often be conflict between the requirements of professional service and this powerful precept of our informal moral codes.

6 *"Be tactful and don't hurt other people's feelings"* and *"Do not deliberately mislead."* Formal codes adopt rigid notions of truth telling, but the informal codes have more complex notions about when to tell the truth and how it might be shaded. The requirement of tact in dealing with other people might be subsumed under the precept "Don't rock the boat," but it is concerned specifically with the problems of candor and truth telling. One is taught early in life not to say or do things that will embarrass or hurt the feelings of others. Informal moralities are more regional than formal moralities and I have found this precept more prevalent and stronger in the midwestern part of the country than on either coast.

Truth telling is still thought of as a good thing in the informal codes, but in many contexts, being too frank is improper. The "white" lie to protect other people's feelings or to further one's own goals is proper, if not essential. Another example, a perversion of the requirement to be tactful, is the technique of spinning now so prevalent in political circles and advertising. One can dress the truth up in ways that, without being an outright lie, gives the most favorable position for the teller without him apparently having to feel guilty for having acted unethically. This practice is at the heart of modern commercial and political advertising.

The problems of truth telling and tactfulness pose difficult dilemmas for the professions. One common problem is how much of the truth a physician should tell a patient about a fatal and incurable disease. Another is the problem of a lawyer who learns in confidence information about crimes that will be of great concern to members of the public.[9] Is he under a duty to disclose or is he under a duty to maintain the confidences? Neither the professional codes nor informal professional moral codes offer very satisfactory guidelines for professionals caught in these complex and difficult dilemmas.

In the modern manipulative world where professionals are often called upon to present the best possible positions on behalf of clients in the courtroom or in business negotiations, there are difficult questions about when trying to shape the truth in its most favorable light to the client crosses the line into outright lying. This is not a situation where bright-lines rules can be used, but the informal moralities, while permitting the tactful lie and the most favorable presentation of a client's case, do have limits that prevent the clear misleading of other parties.

7. *"Share your things."* This is the most difficult part of the informal code to articulate clearly. There is substantial ambiguity about the issue of property rights in the informal code, with potentially risky consequences for professionals. The formal codes are quite clear about the sanctity of private property and the fiduciary responsibility of a professional in dealing with the property of a client. Even the commingling of the professional's and his client's property is forbidden and that is the transgression of the formal code most likely to lead to severe sanctions, particularly for lawyers.

Informal cultural codes say property rights are important, but among friends, family, and neighbors, the appropriation of another's property, if it is not very valuable and you have a need for it, is acceptable. We are all familiar with the child who has received a new toy for Christmas or birthday and wants to keep it to herself. She is told by her mother she should share it with siblings and friends. If she refuses, she is likely to be punished for selfishness.

Generosity is a virtue; greed and selfishness are vices. Since professional ethics are essentially relational, the interesting issue is not the degree to which an actor, whether client, professional, or otherwise, should be generous, but the degree to which the other can expect or be entitled to that generosity.

This informal precept clashes with the formal definition of private property, which is to be protected from unauthorized use by others to the last penny. Jane Jacobs suggests that the Mosaic Law recognized a somewhat more flexible concept of property than our rigid notion of absolute property.

> Moses made a nice distinction between sampling and taking.... It's all right to taste the grapes in a neighbor's vineyard but not to carry them away in a vessel; and it's all right to pinch the heads off some of a neighbor's grain with your fingers but not to bring in a sickle.[10]

We usually state (in public) that the rights of private property are inviolate and stealing a penny is as illegal and unjust as stealing a hundred thousand dollars. In fact, hardly anyone lives by that credo. One important example for professionals is the difficult problem of what, from a strict moral and legal viewpoint, might be termed employee theft. Every employer I have worked for lays down clear and firm rules that company telephones are to be used only for business, not private calls, that copiers can be used only for business, not personal reasons, and that office supplies, such as pens, note paper, and so forth, are not to be taken home for personal use. Most of my colleagues, and I include myself, have violated those rules on occasion. I can think of only one out of the hundreds of employees I have worked with who was scrupulous about paying for all his private calls on the business phone. To the extent it is necessary to excuse such "petty theft" to ourselves or our employers, we make ingenious connections between our personal uses and business purposes. One common excuse is that I do some of my work at home and having the supplies there is justified for that reason. Another frequent justification is that the employee worked overtime or gave more service than was required or paid for by money compensation, so the taking of supplies or services from the employer was an earned right.

Since the employer carries this cost anyway, it would be possible to describe this limited appropriation of the employer's property for personal use as a perquisite of employment. If the reality of minor property appropriation were openly accepted as not being unethical or unacceptable, it would remove certain levels of guilt. As I describe this practice, admit I have done it, and call for recognizing it as acceptable behavior, I am filled with guilt. A realistic ethical code would prevent such a reaction.

A counterargument is the "slippery slope" analysis. If we allow employees some tolerance for appropriating employer's property, they will keep moving the line between accepted and unaccepted appropriation higher and higher. I have never been impressed with that argument because all people, and particularly professionals, are quite good at drawing lines and adhering to them. The important thing is that their lines of acceptable conduct are more flexible and tolerable than the rigidities of a perfectionist ethic.

As long as this matter is not openly discussed, there is no convention or understanding about where the line is or ought to be drawn. The employer, employee A, employee B, and employee C, may all draw them differently. We all would agree there is a major difference between taking home pens and paper on the one hand and taking $300 from petty cash, but exactly where that line is drawn is unclear and should be worked out in conventions publicly discussed and publicly known. The purpose of the appropriation is also important. If we stay with our employee appropriation example, almost everybody would understand the difference between taking home supplies for a mix of business and personal use and taking home supplies to sell to third parties. If the matter of boundaries is left cloudy, the less sophisticated and/or morally venal employees will go over that line, not recognizing the real, instead of theoretical, distinctions people are dealing with. The danger from avoiding more open discussion of these problems is that professionals in dealing with client's property may not be clear about the lines that define the unethical handling of that property.

The ambiguities and difficulties with property relationships illustrate a general problem with informal moral codes. What is their content? These selected precepts and examples show that the informal moral codes are more situation-oriented and flexible in achieving a balance between the wishes of the actor and the rights of others. A complex balancing and weighing goes on. This does not mean, however, that it is acceptable to always and in all contexts prefer your interests over those of others. Teachers of professional ethics needs to be more concerned with the field of informal moralities. That concern should not be primarily to research and articulate the content of the informal codes, although that is not unimportant, but to make students and practitioners aware of the issues, particularly in case of conflicts.

Of these rules, the ones that seem most powerful or most frequently followed in the informal professional code are the requirement of loyalty to your own kind, in this case, the profession, the practice of tact, which permits a substantial amount of shading of the truth, and the celebration of hard work and success.

When one recognizes that there is both a formal and an informal moral code, one sees that confusing signals about both ethical guidelines and the relative weight of each norm are given to professionals, particularly young ones. Excuses may well point to places where the conflict occurs. What was described as the excuse of overriding duty in Chapter 3 is often a conflict between a loyalty prescribed by the formal code and a loyalty under the informal moral code. The excuse "I did it out of kindness" represents a following of the informal moral precept not to hurt other people's feelings and to be tactful.

The informal moral codes because they are seldom carefully examined can also contain contradictions between their precepts. The strong drive to work hard and be successful often conflicts with the precept to conform and not be a troublemaker. Many people in the professions and more generally in the economy are caught between the pressures for success and the pressures to cooperate and exist in social harmony. Nothing in the formal codes of ethics and little in the informal codes are of much help in resolving these fundamental and ongoing conflicts.

Such conflicts and their resolution are hidden because one seldom talks about and almost never appeals to the informal code. Excuses may mask a kind of modern norm conflict, not unlike the traditional struggle between law and morality.

Much social commentary today bemoans the loss of values. The problem is probably the reverse. There is an increase in the number of values we use, some old-fashioned that may seem passé, some that are formally agreed on, some that are used only in a specified group, and so on. The problem is more likely that there is a confusion among a plethora of values, rather than a lack of them. Critics complaining about lack of values often do not like the particular sets of values at work in a particular context and would like to have another set reinstated, usually one that is thought to have worked well in the past. One job of a practical ethics is to sort out these values and develop a way of making choices about the operational scope of each system as well as each particular principle. To the extent that a formal moral code, such as the professional code of ethics, conflicts with an informal social or professional code, it is likely that the informal code will prevail because that is the one learned from and reinforced by the people with whom the professional will deal. But this places practitioners, particularly young ones, in an almost impossible dilemma. When there is a conflict between formal and informal codes, they will be criticized or punished by fellow workers if they do not follow the informal moral code. If there is a complaint about their activity as unethical, they will be judged and sanctioned according to the formal code.

If we are interested in understanding, teaching, or practicing ethics in any complete or practical way, it is clear that we must include a discussion of the informal codes. Without that, one misses many of the real ethical conflicts an actor in our society is always struggling with, often only semiconsciously.

NOTES

1. There is a fascinating, but somewhat dated, discussion of the degree to which the formal ethical code is followed by lawyers in New York City and the degree to which they respond to other moral or nonmoral precepts, such as the opinions of colleagues or clients, in Jerome E. Carlin, LAWYER'S ETHICS: A SURVEY OF THE NEW YORK CITY BAR (New York: Russell Sage Foundation, 1966).

2. The assumption that there is a single morality seems to underlie H.L.A. Hart's analysis in "Positivism and the Separation of Law and Morals, 71 HARVARD.L. REV. 593 (1958), which position is criticized by Lon Fuller in "Positivism and Fidelity to Law—A Reply to Professor Hart," 71 HARVARD. L REV. 630 (1958).

3. Jane Jacobs, SYSTEMS OF SURVIVAL: A DIALOGUE ON THE MORAL FOUNDATIONS OF COMMERCE AND POLITICS (New York: Vintage Books, 1992).

4. Ibid. See particularly the discussion on pp. 63–65.

5. Ibid., p. 64.

6. In a provocative analysis, John Ralston Saul suggests that behind the mask of extreme individuality we profess, the dominant structural and ideological forms of our society are corporatist calling for strict conformity and compliance with corporatist objectives. See John Ralston Saul, THE UNCONSCIOUS CIVILIZATION (Concord, Ont.: House of Anansi Press, 1995). This is a different formulation of what I am here calling a conflict between a formal and informal moral principle.

7. Jane Jacobs, THE DEATH AND LIFE OF GREAT AMERICAN CITIES (New York: Vintage Books, 1961), Chapter 2.

8. Samuel Gorovitz, DOCTORS' DILEMMAS: MORAL CONFLICT AND MEDICAL CARE (New York: Macmillan, 1982), p. 109.

9. One well-known case occurred in upstate New York, where defense lawyers representing a client charged with child molestation learned from their client where the body of a missing girl, which he told them in confidence that he had killed, was located. They checked the site to confirm their client's story and re-

frained from informing the authorities although her parents were frantic with worry. Predictably there was great public outrage when it was learned what the attorneys had done, but they claimed they were under a professional ethical duty not to make any disclosure. The details of the case can be found in Barry S. Martin, "The Garrow Case Revisited: A Lesson for the Serial Murderer's Counsel," 9 CRIMINAL JUSTICE JOURNAL (1987).

10. Jacobs, SYSTEMS OF SURVIVAL, p. 189.

8

The Need to Reformulate Ethical Expectations

We live in a cynical age. A major cause for such cynicism is the apparent absence of ethical behavior on the part of many people with whom we deal. Most of us feel we can no longer trust others, that they will exploit or cheat us, that they may injure us physically out of anger, hostility, or fear, that they will not be available when we need help, and so on. That is a bleak, but not totally unrealistic, view of the contemporary world. Lying behind it, however, has to be a commitment to a set of ethical values that form the basis for those criticisms. We do feel that other people should be trustworthy and supportive, they should deal fairly with us, and they should not hurt us. The notion of reciprocity requires that if we expect those virtues from others, we must in turn also offer the same to them.

Have professionals become less honest, less trustworthy, more materialistic than their predecessors? This is both an empirical and a theoretical question. Our norms of behavior are not only a set of ideals we have, but also the lenses through which we look at and evaluate actual behavior. To what extent should either the actual or the ideal character of professionals be different today than in the simpler world of the nineteenth century?

Excuses may point to a problem—too great a dissonance between actual behavior and our expectations. In much ethical discussion, the assumption is that such dissonance should be eliminated or minimized by changing behavior. In this chapter I want to explore the possibility that our expectations ought to be altered in some ways.

In trying to analyze such disharmonies, there are four important reference points: (1) the actual world of social structure, institutions, and professional culture, that is, the so-called "real" world in which professionals must function, (2) the conduct of individual professionals, (3) the formal professional code, and (4) the informal moral code.

The behavior of professional actors may be out of line with requirements of the actual world. We have grown accustomed to talking about dissonances between human behavior and the needs of the real world. One good example is the way we are polluting the environment and potentially destroying our world. For the professional, the analog would be conduct that destroys the status of professional. If our autonomy is severely restricted or if our expertise and trustworthiness are brought into serious doubt by our conduct so that we are no longer regarded as different from other workers, we will have destroyed our professional world.

Given the degree to which hard realities dictate what people must do to survive and prosper, can the actual behavior we are inclined to label unethical be avoided by decent people? That is a fundamental question that ethical systems must always struggle with.

Another disharmony can arise when conduct may not agree with the formal codes. This is certainly possible, although the formal guidelines are often sufficiently abstract that often there are difficult problems of interpretation before one can say that a particular piece of behavior violates the formal rule.

Professional codes may also be out of harmony with the informal moral code. The last chapter discussed some of the dissonances between the formal and informal moral codes. If the informal moral code is what generally controls conduct, the least dissonance would likely be that between conduct and informal codes. Such disharmonies can, however, occur because the actor may know the informal code imperfectly, may follow the ideal rules rather than the informal ones when there is a conflict, or may just be plainly immoral.

THE GOALS OF REFORMULATING PROFESSIONAL ETHICS

Before trying to reformulate something as complicated as professional ethics, it is important to ask why one should do it and what are the aims or goals of the activity. Over sixty years ago, Lon Fuller and William Perdue wrote:

> We are still all too willing to embrace the conceit that it is possible to manipulate legal concepts without the orientation which comes from the simple inquiry: toward what end is this activity directed? Nietzche's observation that the most common stupidity consists in forgetting what one is trying to do retains a discomforting relevance to legal science.[1]

What they wrote about legal analysis is equally true of ethical analysis. There are a series of objectives we could have. The first is to get the ethical expectations better clarified for practitioners. The second is to make the expectations fit better the contemporary world in which practitioners function. A third is to minimize unethical activity. A fourth is to protect the victims, primarily clients, from unethical activity by professionals. A fifth is to eliminate excessive and unnecessary guilt felt by practitioners.

Are these goals all compatible? One major conflict, shared with the criminal law, is whether the goal of protecting victims requires increasing normative demands and thereby increasing the possibility of more and greater sanctions. In ethics, these sanctions would be greater blame from victims and other observers as well as higher levels of guilt from the actor. In criminal law, that is captured in the sloganizing question: do we protect the criminal or the victim? I suspect that is a false dichotomy. There is no persuasive empirical evidence that strong criminal penalties have in fact decreased the amount of crime. Those who feel that they cannot comply with a demanding system of expectations and consequently will probably be punished under any circumstances are less likely to try to comply.

Which of these goals should be selected? Or rather, from among these goals, which ones should be the weightiest? Being a professional means, or should mean, something more than being an ordinary economic performer. That difference is the explicit commitment to being ethical in a way not required of most market actors. For professional ethics, a minimum goal is to maintain a sufficient level of ethical conduct to retain the status of professional. Of course, just retaining status and privilege is a goal that will appeal only to the holders of such positions, not necessarily to other members of society. Professionals ought to be committed to the view that the exceptional ethical conduct on which that status is grounded provides benefits to all customers and the general public in the quality and trustworthiness of the services received.

A second goal should be to locate the levels of guilt in that range which keeps the ethical system functioning as an effective system of guidance, but not so high as to lead professionals to either ignore the ethical requirements as unrealistic or else become unable to function. In order to achieve this goal, the ethical expectations have to be those attainable in the current work world of professionals.

These twin objectives, (1) maintaining a sufficiently high level of ethical performance to retain the distinctive status of professional, and (2) holding levels of blame and guilt inside the range of effectively motivating performance, are the realistic and important goals for criticizing and reworking ethical expectations.

THE (PROFESSIONAL) WORLD IN TRANSITION

Perhaps the most important way for major dissonances to develop between social reality and ethical expectations is for society to change while the ethical precepts remain essentially the same. It has become commonplace to say we are living in a time of transition, marked by great and rapid social change. But saying, or even understanding, that is far from making the adaptations and alterations in behavior and thought that those changes require. The natural tendency in the face of rapid change is to hold on to traditional ways of acting and thinking as a means of psychological reassurance.

When formulating any norm of ethics that covers a large group or perhaps the entire population, one almost always has in mind a paradigm or model case that one is trying to order. The older model for professional ethics was the small-town general practitioner working in a stable community and enjoying personal as well as professional relations with his clients. The professional ethics we inherited from the nineteenth century were built on such a simple two-person model, which reflected the social reality of that time. Some features of the contemporary professional world, particularly in large urban areas, have changed so much that an earlier ethics might well be viewed as antiquated or of little use in dealing with the kinds of ethical dilemmas professionals now face. We need to start from a newer set of paradigms, which reflects the reality of the situation in which the majority of contemporary professionals practice. Among the changes that must be taken into account are the following:

1. Professionals work mostly in groups, rather than as individual practitioners, and they service many types of clients, often businesses or corporations that embody a variety of interests. Not only does this intensify the possibility of overcommitment, but also of conflicts of interest among various clients. There is also less likelihood of close and long-term relations between professional and client.

2. Professionals are now primarily specialists, rather than generalists. This is one reason for the necessity to group professionals into working teams because it may take a combination of specialists to deal with the particular problem a client brings.

3. The majority of professionals live and work in urban areas rather than in smaller, stable communities. This is caused by a major demographic shift in our population. Professionals are as trapped by it as everybody else. Consequently, there is more alienation. We meet a great variety of people, but enjoy limited relationships with them and only to the extent necessary for the particular item of business or context in which we meet.

4. There is an oversupply of professionals. Most professions have more members than are needed to satisfy the normal demand of the population for their services. Because professionals generally have above average incomes, substantial power, and high social prestige, many young people (and their parents) aspire to reach that level of status and pay. When there is no artificial limit on membership in the profession, the market may be used to eliminate excess professionals, but that process takes time and has great cost in the frustration of those who invest time and money to qualify for the

profession and then cannot make a satisfactory living at it. One problem with letting the market solve this problem of oversupply is that in a highly specialized and technical world, one must prepare oneself for a particular occupation for a long period of time. Shifting not jobs, but occupations at the same level of high status and pay is largely precluded because of the time and cost in preparing for any alternative high-status career.

5. This oversupply of professionals leads to extreme competition inside the professions. The competition to avoid being eliminated at the bottom can be intense, but the competition to be the most successful at the top can be equally or more vicious. In small communities with close-knit relationships, relational constraints would limit carrying ambition and competitive techniques to their fullest extent. Those social constraints no longer inhibit ruthless competition particularly in our large urban areas. Anyone who has been close to professional schools where there is a fierce struggle to graduate at the top of the class because of the important career head start that provides young aspirants, or else watched ambitious young professionals claw their way ahead, will realize how competitive the professional world can be. Professional ethics has had little to say about acceptable types and styles of competition, and yet one of the excuses listed in Chapter 3 is "I had to do it to keep up with the competition."

6. We live in a more manipulative society. Success in life is tied to the ability to manipulate those around you and at the same time to prevent yourself from being manipulated away from your goals and needs. This process begins in childhood since manipulation is often a weapon of the weak against the powerful. Children learn early how to manipulate parents, siblings, and teachers. To get through school successfully, to become a member of a profession, and to get to the top of the profession requires well-above-average manipulative skills. The field that is the art of manipulation par excellence is advertising and it has become pervasive in our culture. For a long time, there was an ethical prohibition against advertising by professionals, but now it has become increasingly common and ever more aggressive. Manipulation cannot be eliminated from human relationships, but one of the goals of ethics should be to put some constraints on how and when it is used. A second field that is highly manipulative is the law, since the common role of the lawyer is to manipulate legal systems on behalf of clients. That, however, is a view that lawyers do not like to take of themselves.[2]

7. Professionals find themselves in more complex and interdependent relationships than did earlier generations. There are the various corporate and bureaucratic organizations they are part of and/or must deal with. They know and do business with many different types of people—neighbors, relatives, close friends, and long-term business partners, but increasingly with people who are all but strangers. The relational constraints, which kept the most exploitative and abusive aspects of human interaction at

bay, do not operate at all when dealing with complete strangers. The emphasis on efficiency, which most people translate as searching for the cheapest product available from whatever source, has also contributed to destroying many long-term commercial relationships.

This growing complexity has made ever-larger groups of people interdependent, which increases the controls on us. As I originally wrote this section, we were living temporarily in a charming little village in upstate New York, where two incidents within one week illustrated some of the problems faced by modern suppliers of service and goods. While neither involved what we would consider as professionals, each helped me understand some of the ethical difficulties being discussed. The first occurred in a laundromat, which served as a collection point for a cleaner. I gave the manager a suit to be cleaned along with a dress shirt to be washed, starched, and ironed. Although the suit came back, the shirt was mislaid. It was ultimately found, but the manager felt terrible and was extremely apologetic. The second involved the town pharmacy, which was asked by the local family doctor to order an unusual medicine for me, which had to be injected on a monthly basis. It is a medicine routinely handled by urologists, but rarely administered by family doctors. There was some urgency, but the medicine was not delivered on time because of an error of the warehouse or truck driver of the pharmaceutical distributor. The pharmacist felt terrible and was extremely apologetic.

In both cases, the persons dealing with the consumer, who liked to think of themselves as responsible independent contractors, performed inadequately in their own eyes even though they had no control over the process that was to guarantee success. Still thinking in terms of simple models, we fasten on the point of contact between provider and customer as the critical place for affixing responsibility, but frequently the provider no longer has any or adequate control over the total performance. We have come to realize this in dealing with the retailer of goods, but are slower to recognize it with the purveyor of services. Our picture of professionals as autonomous experts blinds us to the reality that loss of complete control by the provider is increasingly true of professional services as well.

A good contemporary "professional" example of these problems might arise out of a number of recent commercial airplane crashes in which all the passengers are killed. Quite obviously, one cannot blame the ticket or travel agent who booked the flight. The governmental investigators often have great difficulty in locating the cause of the crash, whether it be some failure in the engineers who designed the plane, in a manufacturer who produced a defective part, in sloppy maintenance produced by carelessness or cost cutting, or pilot error. Any one of these failures could well be caused by unethical as well as illegal behavior, but we have difficulty identifying the particular person that we could blame.

8. While the rapid development of complex and expensive technology has given us a greater capacity to improve services, at the same time it has limited the options we have. Professionals feel strong pressure to use the most highly regarded technology at the time, whatever its cost and whatever doubts the professional might have. As Jacques Ellul has written:

> A surgical operation which was formerly not feasible but can now be performed is not an object of choice. It simply is. Here we see the prime aspect of technical automatism. Technique itself, *ipso facto* and without indulgence or possible discussion, selects among the means to be employed. The human being is no longer in any sense the agent of choice. Let no one say that man is the agent of technical progress . . . and that it is he who chooses among possible techniques. In reality, he neither is nor does anything of the sort. He is a device for recording effects and results obtained by various techniques. He does not make a choice of complex and, in some ways, human motives. He can decide only in favor of the technique that gives the maximum efficiency. But this is not choice. A machine could effect the same operation.[3]

In summary, all these various trends have created or exacerbated ethical problems and extended the dissonances between traditional formal professional ethics and actual behavior by professionals. Professionals or professional groups, however, may not necessarily push to reform the formal ethical principles, even if these standards often do not fit the needs or problems of modern, urbanized, specialized, fragmented professions. An ethical code that does not speak to such problems does not limit professional autonomy. It can then serve as an excuse if clients or others complain of unethical activity.

THE PROBLEM AREAS

Three of the excuses that professionals often use seem to have some validity as justifications. These are the transfer of responsibility, the overriding obligation, and the irresistible pressure. The problems giving rise to these excuses reflect the reality of the way professions are now organized and function, with consequent constraints and pressures on individual professionals. Teachers of professional ethics and mentors must help students understand and adapt to that reality in ways that can be defensible both to the individual's sense of ethics and to the ethics of the profession. Otherwise, there will be enormous guilt carried by professionals and little change in the conduct of the profession as a whole.

The problems pointed out by the three types of excuses are: (1) how we can hold complex teams of professionals responsible for unethical behavior, rather than condemning individual members who cannot control the team, (2) how to handle the multiple obligations of professionals, which make it almost impossible to avoid conflicts of interest, and (3) how to deal with the fact that individuals have lost substantial control over the environment in which they act.

The Responsibility of Professional Groups

When a client hires a professional team to work as a unit in performing a single task, should we, in case of unethical activity, think less in terms of identifying an individual performer at fault and more about the responsibility of the team or the process as a whole? It is easy to argue that the extreme individualism so characteristic of contemporary American thought is descriptively wrong and outdated in the contemporary world. But that way of seeing the world is so deeply ingrained in our culture and teaching that reworking it will be difficult. Looking at disputes through the lens of ethical excuses and legal defenses often points to the clash between strongly held individual rights and the attempt to place corresponding duties on actors who cannot legitimately be held responsible in the interdependent, complex nonatomistic world we live in.

It is not always easy to identify the team or group that could be said to be responsible as an entity. Services are often provided by fluid and complex groupings that are constantly changing. That flexibility is supposed to be a great asset of a market economy. We depersonalize relationships and let people search for the services from the most efficient source. As we become obsessed with efficiency and obtaining goods and services at the lowest cost, we lose much of importance. One is the ability to value the quality of goods or services. A second is personal relationships with others that give a feeling that we deal with a world of suppliers whom we can trust.

It would seem that the answer lies in more cooperative and organic activity by professionals. Jane Jacobs has one character in her book-long dialogue say:

> You said early on that you thought the master virtue, if there is one, is cooperation, because we're social animals. I'll accept that. But cooperation is another two-edged sword. Cooperation turns rancid when it becomes cooperation with immorality or with inappropriate functions and values.[4]

This is important to remember for professionals who are required to cooperate with their clients and with other professionals. That necessary cooperation may blind them to the fact that their clients or their fellow professionals may be engaged in very dubious enterprises. It may also involve them in working with unethical colleagues or clients in complex relationships, which make extricating themselves from the unethical aspects difficult and costly.

There are practical difficulties in moving from an individualist ethics grounded in a simpler and more relational society to one that fits the contemporary provision of professional services. How does one identify a team of providers? A good example might well be the surgical medical team. Here we have a surgeon, several surgical assistants, surgical nurses, an anesthesiologist or two, laboratory facilities connected to the hospital who are on call during the operation, recovery room personnel, and so on. That is a relatively well-defined working team, although there are questions on the fringes, about which additional services of the hospital such as laboratories, X-ray technicians, and so on, also belong to the team. One of the problems the law has had to face in malpractice actions arising from incidents in operating rooms has been trying to identify which of these professionals and support staff are responsible for some professional error. Increasingly, the law has in effect made all of the participants, or more realistically all of their insurers, responsible.

If we abandon fixing responsibility on specific identifiable individuals and instead think of the professional error as one of team responsibility, how do we deal with the consequences? The legal system can do this through the institution of group or joint responsibility and the use of liability insurance. But how does one deal with ethical issues? If there are no ethical, economic, or social constraints on how individual members of the team operate, the amount or the degree of injuries might possibly increase, in which case the cost to all of us as consumers of the team's services, as insurance payers, or as taxpayers will continue to grow and probably beyond the capacity of the society as a whole to carry.

We do know that people working as a unit identify with the group and take on loyalty and responsibility to and for the group. This is a well-recognized phenomenon in team sports and the military. With the right sort of leadership and training, that solidarity can be used to produce not only success, but ethical conduct in the working group.

Since teams are kinds of organisms, can we realistically talk about the ethics of that organism? Obviously one of the issues underdeveloped in contemporary professional ethics and in the broader ethics of the entire society is the ethics of being a member of a team as contrasted with that of being an individual performer and competitor. If one wants to use a sports metaphor, in basketball should one be a good team player piling up assists by letting other members of the team score when they have the better opportunity or should one be a hotshot performer trying to make as many baskets as he or she can? Our current society is ambivalent about this issue and small children receive mixed messages. It gets little better as one becomes adult and qualifies as a professional.

What is probably necessary is to have a two-tiered system of ethics because many professionals, particularly in small communities and at the lower end of the prestige ladder of professions, still practice the way it was done when the formal professional codes of ethics were formulated. Examples are the family doctor, the single lawyer in general practice, the accountant who works for individuals and small businesses, and so on. For them, the concepts of individual ethical responsibility as taught in professional schools still make sense. For those professionals who work in larger organizations, the problem of individual responsibility is more complicated.[5]

Another issue relates to the consequences of unethical activity. This is a matter of blame or of guilt. Obviously, the team *qua* team cannot feel guilt. Its individual members can. But the team can be blamed. In law, it can be held financially liable through the use of insurance. In economics, it can be held liable through withdrawal of patronage or business. Why cannot we speak of the team as being held ethically responsible through blame for its unethical activities? That will become an increasingly important issue into the future as we have larger, more complex, and more integrated professional activities.

Conflict of Interest

Another set of problems exacerbated by the complexity and interdependence of modern society are those discussed under the rubric "conflict of interest." The ethical approach has been to forbid professionals from placing themselves in a situation where they are serving two clients with differing or conflicting interests. It is thought that such a professional cannot loyally serve or represent both interests fairly. Lawyers particularly, but most other professions as well, see the professional as an advocate, representative, or adviser to the particular client and the interests of that client must always be paramount.[6]

Professionals may be asked to fulfill three quite distinct social roles, which require different attitudes about conflict of interest. The first is the role of judge. By role definition, this person is expected to fairly and impartially resolve controversies by applying clear rules and principles. Not only do judges inside the legal system occupy such a role, but also sports referees and commercial arbitrators. Deciding on the basis of personal favor or interest, rather than according to accepted criteria, is a perversion of the role. Recognizing as we now do that one cannot completely eliminate personal biases from influencing decision, this is where we try to avoid the most obvious situations where even decent people might be accused of bias. It is important to maintain not only the expectation, but also the appearance that the judge is fair and impartial.

A second professional role is to be a partisan on behalf of a client. Here the professional should have an overwhelming interest to favor. Having a competing interest may lessen the enthusiasm brought to the task. This has always been a problem for professionals. Being the only lawyer or doctor or accountant in a small town meant that one would constantly have to deal with clients who had adverse interests. Successful professionals who had to maintain relationships with everybody in the town could not be fiercely partisan, but had to consider the interests of others affected by the decision.

This possibility would always lead to the third role, that of mediator who is trying to get the clients to work out their disputes in a way that is mutually satisfactory. Lawyers who move clients toward settlement of law-suits fulfill this role. Clients often approach a professional with the clear understanding that they do not want the professional to be partisan for one or the other nor do they want a judge or arbitrator to resolve the controversy. They need help in working out their difficulties. The professional is supposed to listen, ask penetrating questions, and help them arrive at a mutually satisfying decision. This has always been regarded as a vexing ethical problem in family disputes where more than one family member is consulting the professional. Examples are lawyers in divorce cases, marriage counselors, or doctors hired by a parent to treat a child and who might notice abuse. It can also be a problem for lawyers or accountants hired by a business organization when members of the organization may have competing interests among themselves or with the organization itself.

Professionals may be asked to fulfill any of these three roles and in fact over the course of representing a single client in an ongoing dispute may have to move from one to the other of these roles. Maintaining a rigid ethical attitude of avoiding conflicts of interest is not helpful in guiding such professionals.

One role where conflicts are built in and we have difficulty defining ethical responsibilities is that of the elected legislator. This person is supposed to represent the interests of all members of her constituency, which in large districts covers nearly every interest in the society. She is expected to be fair in deciding what are the predominant interests in the district, then highly partisan in representing those interests in negotiations with other legislators, and, finally, willing to compromise or mediate between various interests to reach results that the larger society can live with. It is recognized that to favor one set of interests because the constituents are wealthier or for values other than public welfare is a perversion of their responsibility, but it is difficult to work out structural rules that will prevent politicians from having to face these issues every day. The ongoing debate about campaign reform and limitations on gifts to politicians shows the difficulties of trying to regulate these problems by structural rules. The best protection is to have decent and fair-minded people who understand the complexities of their competing responsibilities and are committed to being ethical.

We have used too narrow a definition of the conflicts of interest that could raise serious ethical problems. This partly grows out of thinking of professional relationships as a series of one-to-one relations, rather than as a complex web. It is also the product of the strong cultural assumption that the significant motivators in life are always economic or material. Thus, we concentrate on conflict-of-interest situations where one client might pay a professional more than another client and thus influence the decision to the detriment of the second client. Professionals are constantly faced with competing needs or demands by a host of people, only some of which are economic in nature and all of which call for priority rankings and choices. In addition to competing claims by clients, there are claims by colleagues, family members, or the professional's self-interest. Formal professional ethics has largely ignored this complex of competing concerns. The resolution has been left to informal moral codes and personal intuition about how choices should be made.

Ways need to be worked out to unburden successful professionals of excessive and competing duties. Professional ethics must emphasize that nobody should assume more responsibilities in his work world than he can capably and reasonably fulfill. When one hires an eminent surgeon or a famous lawyer, can that professional pass the work off to a less talented or experienced subordinant and still claim the client is receiving his services because of his, often quite limited, supervision? Successful professionals are often over-committed and their ambition or thirst for success encourages them to take on too much responsibility. Ultimately that leads to a heavy psychological and ethical cost to the actor and to diluted services to clients.

Instead of reformulating a set of clear rules trying to define weights of competing claims or forbidding professionals from being caught in such conflicts, it may be wiser to develop processes for resolving this conflict in individual cases, including how to balance the competing claims, notifying the claimants of the potential conflicts, and inviting competing stakeholders to participate in the decision.

The present approach to defining and solving conflict-of-interest problems by eliminating conflicts in certain defined situations reflects a cynicism about the capacity of actors to be fair in making choices. This is largely a modern perception of the power of self-interest in influencing decisions. In 1780, during the trial for treason of Lord George Gordon for instigating the Gordon riots, which destroyed much of London, Lord Mansfield was the presiding judge even though the rioters had destroyed his house and burned his beloved library. " Such is the respect for English courts and English judges, such especially for this great judge, that it did not occur to anyone to question Mansfield's power, even in this case, to hold the scales of justice with an even hand."[7] Lord Gordon was acquitted in the court over which Mansfield presided.

There are limited situations, the judge being perhaps the best example, where it is possible to disqualify the professional and substitute one who is more impartial or appears to be. Apart from such restricted situations, all human beings must make choices between competing claims on a daily basis. Instead of reinforcing the view that they cannot be trusted to make such decisions in an unbiased way, we should educate them in ethical training and normative expectations of the importance of and techniques for doing so as fairly as humanly possible.

Finally, there should be an ethical requirement for assisting the claimant whose interest has to be sacrificed to a weightier claim. He should be notified as early as possible and helped to find alternative professional service.

The Loss of Control over Her Environment by the Individual Professional

Perhaps the single most important political, social, and psychological problem of our time is the feeling of powerlessness in influencing or changing the world we live in. That may be not merely a feeling, but a reality. We are involved in extremely complex economic, political, and communications networks where events happening almost anywhere in the world can instantly change our lives. We talk about one single integrated world, "the global village." The three most potent symbols of this are the multinational corporation, the United Nations, and the Internet. Do we have the choice to opt out of involvement with these complex and huge organizations? Hardly.[8] The process is irreversible and a major contemporary ethical problem is how to guide individuals acting in such complex interrelationships. We certainly do not want to absolve them of responsibility for unethical activity they can control or even influence, but on the other hand it is useless to blame them for matters they cannot control.

This feeling of loss of control by professionals begins at the onset of their career. The first issue for a would-be professional is whether she will be accepted into a professional school for training. While in the school, she will have dreams or hopes about the kind of professional she wants to be and the sort of practice she wants to engage in. She may not, however, find an opportunity in that area. Certainly the field she is in, the types of problems she faces, and the character and style of the people she works with will control her own professional activities and styles. One serious problem today is that those students whose ethical and personal values would incline them toward working with the least advantaged clients are priced out of that possibility because of the heavy load of debt they are carrying in order to obtain their professional education. A substantial income is needed to repay their debts. The salaries governmental agencies, charitable organizations, or poor clients can pay are often too low. A person overburdened with debt is someone who has almost no control or choice over her life in the economic arena. It may be a myth that capitalists or bankers want the people they do business with to be debt free. A debt-free person is one who can choose to act according to her own lights, rather than satisfying her creditors.

In this period of ever-increasing complexity and interdependence, there is much discussion about the necessity to decentralize, which takes the form in politics of returning government to the town and county level, and in business of praise for the small emerging business enterprise (which if it is successful will either become a multinational corporation or will be swallowed up by one).

At the heart of this sometimes bitter dialogue between those supporters of large organizations to match the size of the arena in which they are functioning on the one hand and advocates of small flexible responsive groups on the other is the feeling that we have lost control over our lives. Can local labor unions or small nations effectively counterbalance the power of multinational corporations?

That feeling of loss of power bears a fundamental relationship to the problems of ethics and of ethical excuses. We intuitively feel it is unfair to impose responsibility on individuals who do not have sufficient control to be able to choose how they act. Yet we increasingly feel we do not have such freedom in much of our activities. Is this just another deep-level excuse or is it a realistic appraisal of the lot of contemporary people? That is a vital, but frightening question because if it is answered yes, it throws some of our most fundamental conceptions about ourselves in the gravest of doubts.

At the same time that we feel we are embedded in complex webs of organizations and relationships that increasingly control all our actions, there has been a resurgence of emphasis on individualism and particularly individual rights. This may be a short-term reaction against major social and economic changes. Looking at the world and trying to understand it through the lens of nineteenth-century individualism may inhibit any effective dealing with the changes and problems.

The debate about decentralization indicates the increasingly widespread breakup of hierarchical and rigid institutions as a form of social organization and control. The best example of old-style hierarchical organization may be the army, but they also include large bureaucracies, whether governmental or corporate. In such structures, flowcharts, organizational charts, and job descriptions try to make issues of responsibility and obligation clear. The more flexible and open-textured groupings that modern technology and economy seem to call for in research and development or in making business deals and economic arrangements undercut placing responsibility in stable and knowable ways. If our society is too fluid to make clear identifications of responsibility, there are two major consequences for ethics and law: (1) diffusion of responsibility so those people who do not have real control somehow feel guilty, and (2) people who are damaged may not be compensated because nobody can be clearly identified as responsible for the harm. This second problem has been solved in some fashion either by the liability insurance system or by governmental welfare and insurance programs. The first is an enduring problem of our time. While it cannot be solved by ethical instruction or expectation since it is a structural limitation under which we must function, it should be discussed openly as a problem for professional ethics.

THE PROBLEM OF ATONEMENT OR COMPENSATION

Although the focus of this study is on the excuses that try to establish that the professional cannot be said to have violated professional ethics, there remains an important issue that the law has dealt with and ethics need to consider in more detail. If someone violates the law and injures another, we all feel he ought to compensate the victim for the loss. This is a requirement of compensatory justice. Should ethics also require recompense or, at least, some form of atonement for purely ethical injuries? Should our reformulation of ethical expectations concentrate only on whether there was an ethical violation, or should it also address the consequences of such violation? Is there an ethical responsibility to try to make the victim whole again?

When discussing possible goals for reformulation, I suggested two that are relevant to this discussion: to relieve excessive guilt on behalf of the professional actor and to protect victims of unethical behavior. We feel guilt as individuals. We also are injured as individuals. In the many situations where the particular professional has little or no control over the outcome, should he feel guilt? And, if he feels guilt, how can he relieve himself of that feeling? If he apologizes and that apology is acceptable to the victim, there is relief. If he compensates the victim in some form, there would also be relief of guilt. But there must first be a particular actor who can accept responsibility and an identifiable victim before these steps can be taken. Where identification of responsible actor and injured victim cannot be made, these opportunities for atonement are not open to the professional.

Concern with the issues of blame and guilt for the actor is always appropriate for ethics, but compensation for injured victims should not be a primary concern. In that large zone where ethics and law overlap, legal processes will normally handle the problem of compensation. The zone of importance for ethics is the area of professional autonomy not covered by the law of professional practice. In the zone of autonomy, the protection of victims through the operation of ethics would be through improved practice by ethical professionals.

Relief of excessive guilt, particularly for genuinely ethical people, requires accepting responsibility for misjudgments, carelessness, or sloppy performance. Such release of guilt could be achieved by giving an apology and having it accepted by the victim. It might also come from admitting to professional colleagues, an ombudsman, or others that there was unethical or at least questionable activity and those others then agreeing that the error was in good faith and one that did not rise to the level of violating the law of professional practice and thus is tolerable or forgivable.

One solution to the problem of compensation for victims developed by the legal system has already been discussed. This is the notion of liability without fault placed at the point where it is easiest to spread the cost of the damage among the widest group of consumers of the particular service. This is an insurance device. Out of the group of consumers of a service, those who actually suffer damage will be compensated. The problem with this as a solution to the guilt problem is that it neither identifies a responsible actor nor does the compensation come directly from him. Furthermore, ethical lapses in the zone of professional autonomy are not always easy to quantify so that some form of money compensation can be given. It raises a difficult question to resolve as a matter of social or moral policy: and that is, under what circumstances should the victim not have to accept losses, but be able to transfer them either to a moral wrongdoer or to some pool of funds for compensation?

In this connection, it is interesting that some advisors to the Clinton health care task force in 1993 advocated prohibiting malpractice suits against doctors and only imposing liability on insurance companies and health maintenance organizations, so-called enterprise liability.[9] They justified this proposal on the grounds that such corporate entities would monitor performance by individual practitioners and would cut litigation costs because institutions would settle meritorious claims quicker than individual doctors would. Whatever value this plan might have in containing costs, it could undercut the normative force of individual responsibility for competent and ethical service. But that diminution of individual responsibility may already have been caused by the bureaucratization of much professional practice. It may seem incongruous to talk about the ethical conduct of a law firm, a hospital, a business corporation, or a governmental department, but that may increasingly be our only alternative. This moves us from individual ethics into the area of social justice, leading to the further question whether those aspects of institutional organization that tend to force unethical results by human agents need be altered.

If one has made provision in advance to compensate those who might be injured by professional misjudgments or unethical activity, should that protection excuse the activity so that the professional no longer needs to take blame or feel guilt? Should we reformulate our ethical expectations in situations where it may be difficult to fix responsibility, so that an acting professional should feel no additional responsibility beyond insuring against possible damage? Clearly we want the acting professional to use as much care and competence as possible whether he could be identified as the responsible actor or not. The role of ethics is to encourage that and the means of achieving that is blame and guilt. Would the existence of insurance to compensate victims and the adoption of the view that that is the only ethical responsibility of professionals lead to more careless practice? One of the regular courses I taught in law school was insurance. I often posed the question to classes filled with automobile drivers, all of whom were required to have insurance, whether they felt they drove more carelessly because they were insured and thus would not have to compensate victims out of their own assets. Today most compensation for victims does in fact come from insurance, because uninsured people are almost invariably what lawyers call "judgment-proof," that is, are unable to pay any judgment rendered against them. The students have seldom consciously thought about the problem and we never came to any consensus on whether insurance encourages carelessness.[10]

There is an additional problem with liability insurance as the means to compensate victims of professional injuries caused by unethical practice. Liability insurance evolved to deal with a different problem, the protection of the assets of a person who had or might have been found civilly responsible. Therefore, the court must find the professional acted with legal fault as an essential condition for unlocking the responsibility of the insurer to pay the victim. In the contemporary areas of medical malpractice and manufacturer's liability, the contexts in which absolute liability and an insurance scheme to protect victims are most widely used, this label of illegal activity is a stigma felt by medical doctors and by manufacturers. Obviously, that stigma would not cause guilt unless there was still some confusion about whether the defendant might be said in an ethical and personal sense to be guilty. Their resistance to liability is not primarily because of the cost of the system because insurance spreads those costs widely among the population. The real objection is the necessity of the finding that they acted improperly, which they genuinely resent. This may be another reason why it would be advisable to separate questions of legal responsibility from those of ethical responsibility.

Certainly in those problem areas where it is difficult to affix responsibility on a particular individual or the acting individual does not have sufficient control to act otherwise, then some insurance scheme to protect victims and some way to relieve whatever guilt the actor feels seem necessary. These are tasks that professional organizations or governments can best provide through adequate insurance and through forums where individual professionals can seek advice and absolution for possible unethical activity.[11]

THE PROCESS OF REFORMULATION

When one talks about ethical expectations, it must mean more than just formal codes. A complete account of ethical responsibility includes not only formal and informal moral norms, but excuses as well. Thus, reformulation may require (1) reworking the formal norms, (2) trying to influence changes in informal moral codes, (3) reevaluating the excuses, or (4) changing relationships between any or all of these.

If we are talking about realistic ethical guidelines, it is not sufficient to merely restate the formal ethical system encapsulated in the professional codes of ethics. The real ethical guidelines used by professionals will always differ somewhat from the formal rules of the codes. It is these guidelines that actually control professional conduct. It may well be that those informal, but real, moral guidelines have been changing with the major developments that have been occurring in the past fifty years in our society. Since informal codes are less rigid, they are more easily adapted to change as the need occurs. Unfortunately, without more public discussion and empirical research, we cannot know precisely what the working moral guidelines are or whether they are functioning to achieve ethical goals.

It is a common mistake to assume that students' learning about professional ethics begins with professional school. The norms, particularly the informal codes, are refinements of norms that everyone in the society knows and to which they were exposed in early childhood. The ethical excuses discussed in Chapter 3 are sophisticated versions of excuses regularly used by children. My former secretary, Leslie Vigus, brought this to my attention when she told me she always hears from her two teenage daughters: "You didn't *tell* me I wasn't supposed to do that" or "My sister did it." Courses in professional ethics are expected to undo or reverse ethical training of two or more decades from parents, peers, or teachers, training that has frequently tolerated apparent avoidance of responsibility or accepted excuses that should not work for professionals.[12]

Among the attitudes developed in many children is that as long as one gives an excuse and/or says "I am sorry," everything is all right. If one appears truly repentant, then the consequences of the transgression, whether personal guilt, blame from someone else, or an unpleasant sanction, are unlikely to be imposed and, in their view, should not be imposed. This attitude, cultivated by parents, teachers, and others, helps prevent the taking of responsibility for one's wrongful acts. For mature adults—and how many of those do we really know?—only excuses that are genuine justifications ought to be used to avoid responsibility.

Professional educators, the primary persons who introduce students to professional expertise, often start from the assumption that the student is a blank slate on all matters of professional concern. Students, however, bring all sorts of knowledge about professional activity to school, some of it mistaken, all of it partial. Instead of teaching a new subject, professional ethics, the teacher is only adding another layer on top of personal ethics, social ethics, religious ethics, and informal ethics. The task facing teachers is to weed out inappropriate knowledge brought to school, add new knowledge that belongs to professional expertise and character, and assist students in creating a more informed and useful amalgamation of the old and the new.

When we try to rework professional ethics to take into account the changed environments in which professionals work, it would be unwise to try by fiat or based on purely theoretical analyses to draft a new formal code. One reason is we do not yet know enough about the changing professional world to recognize precisely what is needed. Another is that the formal codes of necessity must be universal and fairly abstract. The serious problems are in their application to the enormous variety of actual problems professionals face.

Instead of legislative enactment, we need a process, somewhat akin to that of common law development, to gradually change our ethical attitudes and to develop flexible and context-dependent resolutions. While the process has to be similar to the centuries-long development of ever more sophisticated legal defenses, we do not have centuries and, given the rapid change of culture, resolutions developed even several decades ago may be obsolete and must be open to adaptation and evolution. At the center of this process, the giving and evaluation of excuses are vital.

To the extent that reformulation involves redefining the scope of what are ethical violations in that zone of professional autonomy not subject to the legal rules of professional practice, what would excuses be like? In discussing issues of character or of virtues when operating in the field of professional autonomy, what kinds of excuses would be considered as justifications? If one compares the ethical excuses in Chapter 3 with the legal defenses in Chapter 5, they track together quite closely, but that would be expected if in fact professional ethics were being defined as a system of rules functioning like a system of law.

The ethical expectations in areas of freedom have to be formulated differently. They are such standards or principles as work to your highest level of competence, be completely trustworthy, respect your clients and others, and so on. When one fails in one or the other of these attempts, the reaction is less likely to be clear and unequivocal blame. Without clear blame, the necessity to make excuses to avoid responsibility may be less compelling. Would not what fulfills the same role as excuses in this area more likely be descriptions explaining what happened, rather than attempts to avoid blame? This raises the issue of whether excuses really belong to or are limited to a rule-based system, whether legal or ethical.

Along with demanding standards of excellence, which call for striving to perform at the highest levels of competence, it is necessary to build in the tolerance that takes into account the fallibility of human beings and the aberrational or nontypical mistakes all of us will on occasion, and we hope rarely, make. That exception cannot be drawn very well on an abstract or general basis. It needs to be worked out in experience and in contexts where the problems arose, the duties were created and then breached, the damage has been done, and excuses or explanations are offered. It is out of the acceptance or rejection of those excuses and the ensuing dialogue that realistic compromises between high demands for performance and recognition of our fallibility will occur.

The analysis of professional ethics that says the problem is lack of knowledge of ethical duties, the assumption that individual professionals always have the option to act in accordance with those duties, and the definition of ethics as establishing borderlines at the outer edges of acceptable conduct prevents us from dealing with the really difficult issues. Such ethical analyses appear theoretical and irrelevant to students and professionals who know or intuit that the most important moral issues they will meet are how to avoid or come to terms with systemic pressures, that is, develop defensible ways of adjusting personal and professional ideals with financial and competitive pressures to compromise.

NOTES

1. Lon Fuller and William Perdue, "The Reliance Interest in Contract Damages," 46 YALE LAW JOURNAL (1936): p. 52.

2. Several years ago, I published a paper, "The Lawyer as Manipulator: Is This a Model for Legal Education?," 31 WASHBURN LAW JOURNAL 506 (1992). It was rejected for publication by what I thought was the most appropriate journal, the JOURNAL OF LEGAL EDUCATION, and when presented as a talk often met a very hostile reaction, even among my faculty colleagues at Washburn University School of Law. Some audiences and readers have been receptive to the ideas there presented.

3. Jacques Ellul, THE TECHNOLOGICAL SOCIETY (New York: Vintage Books, 1964), p. 80.

4. Jane Jacobs, SYSTEMS OF SURVIVAL: A DIALOGUE ON THE MORAL FOUNDATIONS OF COMMERCE AND POLITICS (New York: Vintage Books, 1992), p. 197.

5. The call for a two-tiered normative system may seem incongruous to those who feel that ethical principles must be universal and applied equally to all. Anatole France reminded us of the inequities of a rigidly universal set of norms when he quipped that the majestic equality of the law of France "forbids the rich as well as the poor to sleep under bridges, to beg in the streets, and to steal bread."

6. Increasingly, medical doctors talk about the need to be advocates on behalf of patients with third-party payers, mostly insurers, to see that patients receive the treatment they need.

7. Lloyd Paul Stryker, FOR THE DEFENSE: THOMAS ERSKINE, THE MOST ENLIGHTENED LIBERAL OF HIS TIMES, 1750–1823 (Garden City, N.Y.: Doubleday, 1947), p. 86.

8. In John Ralston Saul, THE UNCONSCIOUS CIVILIZATION (Concord, Ont.: House of Anansi Press, 1995), the author argues persuasively that things like globalization are more ideological than real constraints, but, of course, what we believe is reality is as constraining as any natural constraint.

9. See Robert Pear, "Clinton Advisers Outline Big Shift for Malpractice," NEW YORK TIMES (Friday, May 21, 1993), p. Al, col. 6.

10. One factor that minimizes the problems of controlling conduct is that the driver is the person most at risk for injury in the event of an accident caused by carelessness. Self-preservation would seem to be a stronger motivation for careful

driving than would fear of having to pay a money judgment to some other person who might be injured.

11. Here I am not able in a theoretical study of excuses to consider the very difficult cost questions in such insurance schemes. We already know the cost difficulties that malpractice actions against professionals and the use of liability insurance have produced. There will be difficult problems of identifying what kinds of ethical violations call forth some compensatory entitlement and how much compensation is necessary to be satisfactory.

12. After reading a draft of the article out of which this book evolved, George Hole commented that an important problem is why parents or teachers tolerate such excuses. That question is outside the scope of this book, but it does raise two interesting problems: (1) to what extent excuses are a matter of social or cultural convention, and (2) whether a set of professional ethics can require conduct substantially more demanding than the accepted codes of ethics that control the more general population.

9

The Professional and the Market—Is Efficiency the Predominant Value?

In this chapter, I want to explore why two excuses increasingly given to justify what I would regard as unethical action seem to have such persuasive power. They are: (1) I had to do it to keep up with the competition, and (2) I did not do anything illegal; therefore, I did not do anything unethical. These two excuses taken in conjunction could render professional ethics irrelevant in controlling professional behavior.

In considering whether and how we should reformulate professional ethics, a fundamental issue is the compatibility of market economic theory with the requirements for being an ethical professional. Does the atomistic individualism used in much of the economic and policy analysis of *laissez-faire* or the free-market system fit the concept of professional activity at all? This question leads to a broader issue than the subject matter of this book. What, if any, are the ethics of a performer in a free-market system? Can a person think of herself as a performer in the free market and at the same time be an ethical professional? Is an economic attitude geared toward profit maximization, gaining the largest possible share of the market, amassing the greatest amount of capital, obtaining the most efficient forms of economic functioning, competing in every allowable way for and on behalf of clients compatible with the ethical expectations we associate with being a professional?

THE POWERFUL HAND OF THE MARKET

It is now widely, but not universally, accepted that economies in North America, if not the entire world, ought to be built on and/or evaluated solely on market economic theory. Individual performers are seen as being subject to market forces, the law of supply and demand, the necessity to be competitive, the goal of greater productivity, the need to acquire capital, and so forth. Professionals who themselves are major performers in the market and are the principal advisors to other and even more significant market players are not free, according to this theory, to escape market pressures. That arises out of what has become in our time almost an obsession with the importance of efficient, productive, profitable, and cost-contained commercial activity.[1] In their preprofessional and professional education, most contemporary professionals have been steeped in free-market ideology. And yet professional ethics as traditionally understood requires them to act differently from other performers in the market. Neither economic theory nor professional ethics deals adequately with this clash of values.

There are a few core values at the heart of our social thinking and practice. Among them are justice, cooperation, stability, equality, freedom, and efficiency.[2] There have always been tensions among these various central values and how they ought to be balanced and implemented. Ethics belongs primarily to the realm of justice, which decreases in importance as efficiency ascends. In the ongoing balancing of values, a strong emphasis on efficiency at all costs means a lowering of the importance of the values of justice, cooperation, stability, and equality. The impact on freedom is more difficult to assess. It is part of the free-market ideology that relying on the market is protective of and consonant with freedom for the individual actor. Obviously the poorer segment of our population with little or no capital do not enjoy much freedom in the market. The more successful economic competitors might be said to have increased freedom, but the requirements of the competitive game do not allow them much scope for other goals or choices than efficient production.

It is important to grasp how all-encompassing the value of economic efficiency has become, even for professionals. Professional ethics is based on the notion that professionals are a separate category from all other workers and that a part of the justification for that distinction is that they are committed to a different and more demanding set of ethical obligations. In creating the special category of professional, one could base it on distinctions between the technical skills and knowledge that professionals possess and those held by ordinary workers along with differences in compensation and social prestige. When professionals are required, however, to defend the privileged position held by in the work world, they have always emphasized the ethical dimension. As the two excuses mentioned at the beginning of this chapter indicate, there is now serious doubt about whether there are significant differences in ethical practices between normal economic performers and those who call themselves professionals.

Some people take the position that the market mechanism, Adam Smith's famous invisible hand, is empirically true and no economic actor can escape its regulation. A greater number believe that it is the best of the range of economic systems for a culture and political system to select. Whether it is necessary to take either position, and I am dubious about both,[3] it is clear that a substantial majority of Western economic actors now accept one or the other of these variants. This belief becomes a part of the reality we must all live with.

Professionals obviously are a part of the commercial world and subject to all the material and intellectual forces that influence or control economic activity. Whether as individual practitioners or as integrated members of larger economic enterprises, professionals are viewed as subject to market forces and the demand to be efficient, to control costs, and to make profits. Not only are they perceived as subject to these social or economic forces, but increasingly much of their analysis and thought about what they are doing and the myriad of daily choices they face are made in the framework developed for the business community. While most professionals would resent being categorized as business people or just another class of workers or entrepreneurs, it is increasingly difficult to discern differences in their behavior or thought from that of "mere" business people.

MARKET-DRIVEN ANALYSIS

Professionals are economic actors. Those professionals, such as lawyers, accountants, or engineers, who advise business people on how to conduct their affairs must be prepared to think and communicate in the terms used in commercial analysis. In addition, professional practices are businesses themselves. In an ever-increasing service-oriented economy, professionals become a more central part of the economic system. Professionals can in theory work with two separate analytical systems, the one they use with clients and a different one they use in making their own professional decisions, but in practice that flexibility in moving back and forth between analytical frames is difficult for most people to achieve. Even medical doctors, whose primary professional concern is not economic activity, but matters of physical and psychological health, are now caught in the pressures of cost containment and efficient delivery of services to their patients. Teachers who have traditionally thought of themselves as above personal economic concerns are caught in an environment requiring efficient delivery of their services and the development of ways to measure those services in order to satisfy whoever is responsible for funding educational activities that they are getting their money's worth.

Neoconservative economic theory requires a certain type of professional ethics, one that can be fitted into the calculus of the rational maximizer of his own interests. This rational actor is, of course, a theoretical, rather than a real, person. The assumptions about economic actors are that they are rational, well informed, have enough capital to participate in the market and are concerned only with maximizing their utilities. They are supposed to have choices about what their utilities are and how they will live their lives, but the assumptions of the theory are that all the significant motivators are economic and that we all want to increase our profit or share of material goods. If such persons exist in the real world, they must be able to identify and assign a value to each interest or factor, which must be taken into account. If ethical conduct is one such factor, it must be given a value, or quantified. Quite clearly in the weighing of a cost-benefit analysis or a utilitarian calculus, ethics is not valueless, but the central question is just how high a value is placed on it by the actor, or by the outside world when it reacts to unethical activity. In the real world of commercial activity, the assigning of a quantity or weight to the ethical option is not done objectively, but subjectively by the individual actor. If it is done by a self-interested economic performer, the tendency will be to assign a relatively low value to the ethical option with its attendant costs.

Not only in economic theory, but also in business activity and in political and taxing policy, there is almost total emphasis on lowering cost, on increasing productivity, on raising profitability. "Bottom-line" or "cost-benefit" analysis (simplistic utilitarianism) is the way almost all professional students are now taught to think, so much so that it has become almost unconscious, second nature to them. When faced with a choice situation where a decision must be made, the actor lists all the benefits or income from each decision, then all the costs or expenditures from that same decision. The one that produces the highest level of benefits or profits is deemed the best or soundest decision. The notion of efficiency is commonly translated into reducing the cost side of the equation as far as possible, which will then produce higher profit levels. In making such calculations, every factor has to be quantified. This means intangible values are likely to be either ignored or vastly undervalued.

What are some examples of the pervasiveness of efficiency as a dominating value in the professional (and economic) world? For business people (and their professional advisors and employees), downsizing, moving plants, and cutting production costs at the expense of workers, communities, and often product quality. For medical care, the development of HMOs, the elimination of many hospitals and medical services, and lack of insurance for high-risk patients. For the law, the adoption of efficiency criteria for resolving problems and deciding cases as advocated by the law and economics movement. For politics, the importance of cutting taxes, limiting social programs, and cutting deficits.

My primary interest is not to discuss these matters prescriptively because my personal preference for balancing these core values is quite different from the accepted economic wisdom. I am making a descriptive statement about the world in which my colleagues and my students live. Or more accurately, I am describing the world they perceive they live in. Within that dominant framework, what are the consequences for ethical theory and teaching? Even if I wish that my students and most people in my world used a different set of lenses to see the world and to make choices, that dominant view is an attitude I must relate to when I communicate with them.

One caveat needs to be made here. I do not contend everybody has accepted this way of seeing the world and making decisions, merely that it is by far the most common and dominant form of analysis. The highest percentage of dissidents from this worldview may well be teachers of professional ethics because it is difficult to do the job this role demands once one accepts the efficiency-dominated model.

THE COSTS OF ETHICAL BEHAVIOR

Since efficiency requires the delivery of services at the least manageable cost, are there costs associated with acting ethically? And if so, how should those costs be quantified or weighted in making the efficient business decision?

One cost is the forgoing of opportunities, particularly the use of inside information. A clever businessman is one who has the best sources of information about where the opportunities are for making money. Professionals, particularly lawyers, accountants, or investment counselors, will inevitably learn from clients information that has great value. We also know about the widespread extent of commercial espionage, the gathering of information by aggressive business performers from competitors about technological or business innovations. Much of that knowledge is held by professionals who work for the competitor and it is worth a large amount of money. Professionals also learn in advance about what is likely to happen and that can be a valuable investment tool for their personal accounts. If they are believers in maximally optimizing their opportunities, why in the contemporary frame of analysis should they not use it to enrich themselves? The ethics we teach may be a weak bulwark against that temptation.

Another temptation is to pad expenses or furnish questionable or unnecessary services?[4] What an individual professional has to sell, besides her technical expertise, is her time. It is difficult for a client who is hiring a professional to determine whether that professional's expertise is the best and how much time was necessary in order to perform the job. If the professional claims to have performed services that she did not do, or that the services took more of her time than in fact they did, that deception is hard to detect. A competitive market is not adequate to regulate this because the client has no opportunity to have the particular service performed elsewhere in order to make comparisons. Since many professional services are not standard or routine, other people's experience may not be a useful guide. Presumably the protection the "market" expects and offers is an informed consumer who will know if the quality of the service or product is worth the price paid. But in the professional-client relationship, the client is hiring the professional because it is a service or knowledge he himself does not have or cannot perform for himself. So how should he judge whether he is getting his money's worth?

The other side of the coin of time costs from exaggerating the value of services is the pressure to cut service by sloppy preparation or by putting too little time and concern into handling a client's problems. Cost cutting has become a way of life in the contemporary economic world and one way to cut costs is by spending less time on each client's affairs. If sloppy or careless procedures take less time and the probabilities of that affecting the result are perceived by the professional as unlikely to occur or to be detected, efficiency would seem to require that unnecessary time not be spent to ensure that no mistakes are being made.[5]

Closely allied to this is taking on more clients than the professional can adequately handle. The consequence has to be careless performance and short cuts to obtain results. Income will increase, but inevitably costs per unit of work will also have to decline, and as a consequence profits will grow, so this appears to be an efficient course of action, but clearly one of questionable ethics.

The temptation that is the easiest to resist is to misuse a client's funds or to obtain a client's property by fraud. This is simple to define in terms of wrongdoing, probably easiest to detect, and thus has been made illegal or criminalized. The penalties, when such misuse of a client's property is discovered, are quite severe. Converting a client's money will almost always lead to losing one's professional license. It can also lead to civil or criminal legal penalties. Still, such misuse of a client's funds happens more often than one would like or expect.

While it is common in chamber-of-commerce-type rhetoric to claim that good ethics is good business, ethical conduct above a minimum level of legal compliance is not commercially efficient. It always carries costs in time spent with clients and in forgoing opportunities to make profits. This makes ethical activity inefficient, particularly in short-run calculations. One can make the argument, and I often have, that good ethical conduct and the reputation that accompanies it will in the long run produce more success for the professional (and the businessman) than immediate cost-minimizing efficiency. Contemporary commercial attitudes, however, downplay long-range analysis in favor of short-term profits. The stock market and its evaluation of the worth of each entrepreneurial institution in terms of last quarter's profits does not encourage long-range thinking on the part of commercial actors.

HOW TO AFFECT BEHAVIOR IN MARKET ANALYSIS

If professionals are rational maximizers of their own utilities and they make the market calculation for each choice of action they take as professionals,[6] the only way to change their behavior would be to change the factors going into the calculation.

One could, in theory at least, increase the rewards of ethical action so the ethical option would be more profitable than the unethical one. This technique is sometimes used in the business world, when governments give subsidies or tax breaks contingent on the businessperson or entity acting in ways that public policy favors.

In our cultural ethos, which has a bias toward using punishment to change behavior, it appears more plausible to work with the cost side of the equation. If one accepts the efficiency paradigm, the only workable tactic is to increase the cost of unethical activity so that it is no longer profitable. But the consequences of unethical action are blame and guilt, notoriously difficult concepts to quantify and to increase as a matter of social calculation. In an efficiency analysis, the cost has to be economic (or arguably imprisonment) since all the other factors that go into a cost-benefit analysis are economic.

To change the rational analysis that goes into business planning, one must lay down precise rules about acceptable conduct and price the consequences for violating those rules high enough to make such violations unprofitable. Not only must the cost be sufficient to deter conduct, but the probabilities of discovering the violation and imposing the costs must be sufficiently great so that the rational economic performer has to take them into account.

It is possible to define with precision unacceptable conduct at the margins. This, however, tends to be the territory of the law, rather than ethics. As one moves into areas of autonomy or choice, the area I believe is the true domain of professional ethics, it is very difficult to describe with precision the line between acceptable and unacceptable behavior.

Then it is necessary to find suitable negative consequences that can be quantified and attached to the unwanted action. The traditional sanctions for unethical conduct, such as blame or guilt, do not meet these criteria.

To understand the breadth of the problem that efficiency analysis poses for professional ethics, we cannot work with the concept of professional ethics that is dictated by that framework. We need as the basis of our critical evaluation to consider a broad definition of professional ethics that includes aspirational ethics and ethical guidelines inside the areas of autonomy or freedom of choice. Efficiency analysis defines these ethical issues as outside the concern of professional morality. It is, however, precisely in this area of autonomy where traditional ethics seeks to motivate professionals to aspire to excellence in performance and to maintain exceptional degrees of trustworthiness.

THE DILEMMA FACING TEACHERS AND MENTORS OF YOUNG PROFESSIONALS

As a long-time teacher of professionals and a person concerned with ethical issues, there are a series of questions that I and others like me need to face: (1) Is the analytical system of neoconservative economic theory compatible with professional ethics as we normally teach it? My view is that it is not. The only way we can make them compatible is to narrow and legalize professional ethics. (2) What percentage of educational time and effort are devoted to instilling these two quite different systems into young professionals? Substantially less for ethics than for utilitarian decisionmaking aimed at economic efficiency, particularly if we take into account informal education and socialization by news and entertainment media. (3) What amount of time in formal or informal professional education is spent in trying to reconcile the difficulties in these two systems, not merely as a formal method, but as a problem that must be solved on a daily basis by acting professionals? Relatively little, because ethicists usually give a theoretical, rather than a practical, answer. (4) Are professional ethics formulated in a way that would make it possible for them to fit into a cost-benefit or utilitarian analysis; that is, are the rules clear and the penalties predictable? A related question is whether professional ethics ought to be formulated in that particular way. (5) Is the current emphasis on professional ethics primarily a public relations or marketing effort to try to persuade the public at large that professionals are ethical and trustworthy? Or is it a serious effort to try to raise the level of ethical performance by professionals? (6) Why does the general public have such a cynical view of professionals and their ethical behavior? Is it because ordinary citizens have not been adequately trained to accept neoconservative economic analysis to believe that efficient solutions are also ethical ones? Or do they believe that professionals are required to be efficient, rather than ethical? (7) Is the almost exclusive definition of professionals as technically competent individuals and the strong emphasis on that aspect in professional education a way of avoiding the dilemmas and tough choices in these issues? All these questions need substantial exploration.

Such questions, however, ought not to be viewed as academic ones to be answered definitively as a matter of theory. They ought to be at the heart of all formal and informal education preparing people to be professionals. Each professional must answer them for himself or herself and the answers will vary depending on the values each one brings to the problem contexts.

The most important of these questions, particularly for individual professionals, is the problem of how the tension between the efficient operation of their business is to be balanced with the requirements of ethical, fair, and just performance. The balance both socially and individually has become lopsided by the obsessive stress of economic objectives of growth, profits, and efficiency.

Professionals and students aspiring to be such can be said to fall roughly into three groups on this issue of efficiency versus morality. The first group at one end of the continuum are essentially amoral, that is those whose criteria for choice are crudely utilitarian and self-interested, the ones whose only method of choice is that dictated by the efficiency paradigm. At the other end of the continuum are those who are basically decent persons for whom moral criteria of choice are very important. Where they got their tendencies toward making the moral realm central in their personal and professional choices is an interesting and important question, but they probably bring it to the profession, rather than having it instilled by professional education. The middle group are those who are both self-interested and moral, that is to say, are clearly caught in the ongoing tension between the two camps.

I do not know the percentages that belong to each group, but it is substantial for each. The largest group is the middle group, and they are the interesting and important group for professional educators to look at. Our ethics instruction tends to reinforce or at least permit the amoral group to do nothing other than make a self-interested efficiency analysis. Nor does our instruction probably move those inclined to be moral away from that tendency. In other words, I assume that formal professional ethics training has little impact on either group at the ends of the continuum. For the middle group, the bulk of our students and practitioners, the danger is that professional education as well as the dominant cultural attitudes tend to push them into the amoral group. We talk as if they (and their clients) are entitled to be self-interested maximizers of their own interests. If our responsibility is to give them other rules of choice for guidance, do we do that? If our responsibility is to help them see the pitfalls in self-regarding action, do we do that?

Each group represents a different kind of balance of the tensions. The amoral group is probably not totally indifferent to morality, but the balance has swung so far toward efficiency that their moral tendencies have little or no impact on their choices. The moral group is not totally indifferent to the need to be productive and efficient, but that is not the dominating value for them. The middle group is probably confused about the tensions and has not worked out any good way of integrating or balancing these tensions. For people who are unsure and unable to live in an ambiguous world and who are seeking fairly clear and simple rules, efficiency criteria can seem to offer a solution to these difficult tensions of the world we live in.

If we must develop a formal code of professional ethics that speaks to all three groups, or try to teach the whole range as if they were a homogeneous collection of people, there is a serious problem of choice. If our code is aimed at the amoral group, presumably those whose lack of ethical concerns will cause the most problems for the profession, it requires a highly legalistic code defining serious border crossings and totally unacceptable behavior, followed by serious, quantified, and reliable punishments[7] If, on the other hand, we focus on the middle group, the instruction and codes should have quite different purposes. The codes should encourage professionals to weight the tendency toward use of moral criteria heavier and to help develop guidelines and priority rules when they are caught between the pressures to be efficient and at the same time to be decent.

Teachers are, of course, professionals and must admit that their world is increasingly dominated by efficiency analysis. We are not merely observers of the way efficiency analysis works for our students and for the professions. We are also trapped by it. One indicator of this is the degree to which our analytical frames are also those of economic analysis. The second is the percentage of our time spent teaching technical competence and that spent teaching ethics. The consumers of our products, those who hire professionals, are concerned with the technical competence of our students. They are less concerned with how ethical the students are. They do want the students to be able to avoid the pitfalls of being caught out in unethical action. Much ethical instruction is about how to *appear* to be ethical, that is, how not to get caught.

Presumably teachers as both professionals and functioning humans fall into the three groups of people who have balanced the tensions between ethics and morality in the differing ways. I would assume that those who fit the amoral group for whom efficiency is the most important are least likely to find themselves in the formal teaching of professional ethics. They are more likely to concentrate on mastering and teaching the technical skills of the particular profession. Those from the group who are basically moral and decent will have a disproportionately high representation among the teachers of professional ethics. This raises interesting questions of the degree to which they can relate to, understand, and communicate with those who fall into either the amoral or the middle group.

What options face teachers of professional ethics? There are three basic choices. The first is to accept the overriding importance of market economics for professional as well as commercial players. This is not only a descriptive problem; that is, is this the way the contemporary professional world works and contemporary professionals think? It also poses a prescriptive problem. Should we develop and teach an ethics that fits that reality? If so, then we can work on an underdeveloped problem. What are the appropriate ethics, if any, for performers in a market economy? The answers to that will define the ethical expectations not only for economic players, but for that subgroup who think of themselves as special, the professionals. To the extent that we think some types of conduct are unacceptable under that paradigm, we would then have to define those expectations in clear terms and place a sufficiently high price for violating those expectations that it will affect the bottom-line choices of actors. That will be difficult to do in practice because both market economics and professional ideology place great value on freedom from outside regulation and, with their great economic and political power, economists, business people, and professional organizations resist mightily any efforts at restricting that freedom.

The second option is to fight the paradigm and to suggest that it so underemphasizes important social values, such as justice, community, cooperation, and long-term rational planning, that no decent professional, ordinary worker, or citizen can operate on that basis. There are some indications of such a counterrevolution in the works, but to be successful, it must be more than merely a mention in a special course in professional or personal ethics. Rather, it must be carried to all public analysis in the classroom and in the media that affects the way that people think.

Our third option is to continue the present course of teaching a theoretical set of professional ethics that are not always practiced by professionals because of economic or social pressures. We can accept the reality of the legalization (and trivialization) of professional ethics and go through the motions of teaching them as if they mattered. We can try to affect the more egregious kinds of unethical professional activity by laying down clearly defined rules about unacceptable activity and attaching severe penalties to them. We then have to ensure that in fact the penalties will be incurred by unethical professionals. Taking that approach is selling out to the conservative economists.

There is obviously an expectation and a need for the public to believe that professionals are ethical and trustworthy, at least more than their perception of the worst aspects of commercial dealing, such as the used-car salesperson. The current emphasis on formal professional ethics training, the hiring of ethics specialists to advise corporations, the codes of ethics adopted by the professions are all efforts to cater to this expectation. Rather than a serious voice for more ethical conduct, we are in danger of becoming a public-relations enterprise, that is, to proclaim that ethical professional activity is the rule, when that may not be true. It is important not to forget, in Stephen Toulmin's words, "usual hypocrisy responds to the perceived demands of respectability."[8] Do we want to participate in that hypocrisy?

THE HARD AND UNPLEASANT CHOICE

Which horn of the dilemma described in the preceding section should we select? Should we abandon any ethical expectations for professionals that are incompatible with the ethical limitations placed on the most competitive performers in the free-market arena? From my somewhat cynical viewpoint, the ethics currently practiced in the marketplace means only that one not do anything illegal that could lead to serious penalties or associated costs that cannot be passed on to consumers. This would bring us back to the increasingly widely used excuse in the political and commercial realm, "I did nothing unethical because I did nothing illegal." The position that a professional can in the moral realm be nothing more than a free market performer abandons all that being professional means. However, it would, at the practical as well as the theoretical level, solve many of the real internal human conflicts that professionals are exposed to. If our dominant goal were to relieve (excess) guilt from professionals, this would be the most effective path to take. Scholars and teachers of professional ethics would then be free to devote their energies to the important question of what are or should be the ethical limitations, if any, on market performers in the contemporary economic system.

The other horn of the dilemma is to insist that the concept of professional is now, as always, an extremely important one for the society and the economy. That means that professionals whom we entrust with our important affairs must be trustworthy, committed to high levels of performance well above mere competence, and devoted to the interests of their clients above their own interests. If that is the horn we select, we cannot accept the two excuses that my competition is acting unethically, therefore I must be permitted to do so, and the only ethical injunction I must respond to is not to be caught in illegal activities.

Every professional and aspiring professional faces this choice on a regular basis, whether they are aware of it or not. And whether the status of professional and the practice of true professional ethics continue depends not on a theoretical answer, but on the practices of individual professionals in their daily activities.

NOTES

This chapter owes much to the inspiration of Hans Mohr, who in a casual conversation made the assertion that "professional ethics are inefficient." He was being critical of contemporary attitudes and that started me thinking about the problems in this chapter.

1. This is not a new phenomenon because modern intellectual thought has always been captivated by economic analysis, although the obsessive quality is much more marked in recent decades. See Stephen Toulmin, COSMOPOLIS (Chicago: University of Chicago Press, 1990, 1992), p. 125:

As for the "human sciences ": many English people are suspicious of them to this day. Anthropology was fortunate: it began as an offshoot of Colonial administration. Sociology was under a cloud in England until at least 1960. Only *economics* flourished, beginning in Adam Smith's Scotland as an aspect of moral philosophy, and achieving mathematical exactitude in Cambridge without losing its philosophical roots. Alfred Marshall was a philosopher at first, John Maynard Keynes was a student of G. E. Moore, while Anglo-American economic theory stayed firmly on the "reason" side of Cartesianism. Economics did not explore the *causal* tangle of motives or feelings behind real human choices, exploring instead the *rational* choices of "ideal" producers or consumers, investors, or policymakers. For the purpose of economics, "causal" factors were set aside, in favor of ever more precisely "rational" calculations. In this way, modern proprieties were protected in the life of the intellect, as well as in respectable English society.

2. See John Rawls, A THEORY OF JUSTICE (Cambridge, Mass.: Harvard University Press, 1971), p. 6.

3. It should be clear from the discussion that I am not a passionate believer in the efficacy or the inevitability of free markets. For a clear presentation of my thoughts on this matter, see Banks McDowell, DEREGULATION AND COMPETITION IN THE INSURANCE INDUSTRY (Westport, Conn.: Quorum Books, 1989), particularly Chapter 2.

4. This is the problem I explored in Banks McDowell, ETHICAL CONDUCT AND THE PROFESSIONAL'S DILEMMA: CHOOSING BETWEEN SERVICE AND SUCCESS (Westport, Conn.: Greenwood Publishers, 1991).

5. For a suggestion that sloppy preparation and performance is a very serious, if not the most serious ethical problem for lawyers, see David Luban, LAWYERS AND JUSTICE: AN ETHICAL STUDY (Princeton: Princeton University Press, 1989), Introduction, p. xxv.

6. This theoretical assumption is highly dubious as a descriptive statement for the way any real human being with his complex set of motivators actually makes choices for action.

7. This development seems to have occurred in the legal profession as it moved from an essentially aspirational Professional Code of Ethics to a more rule-oriented Code of Model Rules.

8. Toulmin, COSMOPOLIS, p. 163.

10

The Responsibility of Others toward the Excuse Giver: The Need for Dialogue

Professional ethics is a relational subject defining how professionals ought to treat others. A professional must be concerned with how she acts and is acted upon. As a customer of other professionals, she can become a victim of unethical activity. Under the principle of reciprocity, she should not expect ethical performance from others unless she is willing to give it in turn. When a professional takes on a task, she should do it to the best of her ability; if she makes a promise, she should perform it if at all possible; if she receives a confidence, she should keep it private. These important rules of conduct are often overlooked when one is the actor and seldom missed when one is the victim.

Sometimes there will be a justifiable reason why the professional cannot perform a duty she has assumed. She should not be ashamed to raise such an explanation (excuse), but must be convinced it is valid. The best test is whether it does persuade others or, at least in her best judgment, is likely to persuade others. If she does not test that out by discussing it with the client or objective bystanders, she can never be sure she is not playing games with herself and merely avoiding responsibility. The obligation to perform ethical duties contains an obligation to rely only on excuses she is persuaded have validity.

When the professional is victim, he is entitled to expect others to perform their duties to him. As victim, he is the one most interested in assessing the validity of any excuse given. This process of receiving excuses and assessing their validity is a constant in daily living. Its breeding ground is the relationship between parent and child. Not only does the parent or other infant caregiver begin the process of instilling the ethical expectations of the culture, but the parent must also assess whatever excuses are given by the child, usually in an attempt to avoid punishment. For some parents, this acceptance or rejection of excuses is done capriciously depending on the parent's mood or other extraneous factors, so the child comes to believe there is no reason or consistency in parental evaluations of his excuses. By the time the child is five or six, this role of accepting or rejecting his excuses is supplemented by teachers, school principals, neighbors, as well as peers. I would like to say there is less capriciousness in the judgments of teachers or school principals than in cases of some parents and peers, but a long lifetime of dealing with both makes me cautious about making that claim.

Not only may each professional be actor or victim, but also an observer of the interactions between others in his immediate vicinity. One strong informal principle in our society is that there is something questionable about intervening in the relational problems of others. That has permitted bystanders to watch abuse of children by parents, violent rapes, and physical attacks without any overt reaction. "Don't get involved" is both a strong and a dangerous cultural attitude. Just as the professional should have an opinion about the ethical quality of his choices as an actor and more likely an opinion about the ethics of those whose actions impinge on his life, he should have such opinions about actions he observes between others. The problem is not whether one has such opinions, but how he should act on those opinions.

I have been critical of the utility of the two-person model as an analytical device in contemporary professional ethics because it leads to oversimplification of complex relationships. That criticism is important when dealing with duty and breach. Is it as valid when thinking about ascription of responsibility and the ethical consequences of blame or guilt? Excuses are given to avoid blame. If the consequence of an ethical breach is internal to the actor, the excuse may be given by the professional to herself to assuage or avoid accepting guilt. If a victim has suffered damage and blames the actor, the excuse will be given to the victim. If an observer has watched the action and finds it unethical, the excuse will be given to escape the condemnation or disapproval of that other person, particularly if he is important to the professional. If the excuse works, it will minimize or eliminate the guilt, blame, or disapproval. If unpersuasive, the consequences remain. This chapter looks at the ethical relationship primarily from the point of view of victim or observer. Any excuse, if it is to be a justification, ought to be acceptable to all these: actor, victim, and observer.

Does a victim or an observer have ethical obligations about how he evaluates an excuse? Must he be objective? Must he try to place himself in the shoes of the actor and understand her motives and the pressures she was responding to? Such impartiality and empathy is clearly easier for an observer than for a victim to achieve. The giving of unjustified blame is an act that can cause damage. The victim who blames another has in that judgment become an actor and must assume the ethical responsibilities of one whose activity can harm another.

While modern life is highly organized and controlled by complex systems, we still relate to each other primarily as individuals. We interact in very small groups and most commonly in one-to-one relationships. It is there that most excuses are given and either accepted or rejected. The giving of excuses and the open discussion of their validity should help us to understand ourselves, others, and the problems that we all face in a society in transition.

Whether there is a duty, whether there has been a breach, and whether an excuse works are clearly dependent on context and the relationship between the people involved. When I talk about other people accepting or rejecting excuses given by an acting professional, I want to distinguish types of relationship. Since my concern is professional ethics, one party to any of these relationships will be a professional or a student in a professional school. There are four types of relationships with different problems. The first is the teacher or mentor relationship. The second is that of peers, which in the context of this discussion would be with another professional. Third, there is the victim, the one who receives harm from the actor's arguably unethical act. Finally, there is the observer of such an act who is neither a mentor nor a coprofessional. For celebrity professionals, the observer could even be the public at large. All of us are naturally concerned with what our neighbors, family members, and friends think of us.

The initial relationship is that of professional teacher or mentor to the novice aspiring to be a professional. He is the one who first formally prepares the student to be a good technical expert and hopefully an ethical performer. Many professional educators view their responsibility as primarily, if not solely, to impart the profession's technical expertise. In recent decades, they have reluctantly come to realize that their former students when practicing as professionals are increasingly regarded as amoral, if not immoral, by the public. As a consequence, specialized courses in professional ethics have been added to the curriculum. These often do little more than teach the content of the professional code of ethics.

I have argued elsewhere that every professional teacher has two additional ethical responsibilities.[1] One is to point out in every discussion of technical expertise when an ethical issue or dilemma may be present and discuss what the proper resolution might be. This helps prevent a sincere, but unacceptable excuse, which is that the professional did not recognize there was an ethical problem. The second responsibility is to serve as a model of professional character, that is, to set an ethical example in the way he performs his duties in relationship to the students. One important aspect of this modeling is to show how the professional teacher makes ethical choices in difficult situations. He also must often give persuasive excuses when his students feel they have been treated unfairly.

Now I would add a third ethical responsibility to the teacher's role, which relates to excuses. The teacher may vary in the degree to which she allows the student great autonomy or whether she sets precisely defined tasks.[2] To the extent that a specific task is set out, the teacher has an obligation to consider seriously any excuses the student offers for not performing the task promptly, fully, and competently. Should the excuse not be persuasive, that needs to be made clear to the student. This provides an excellent opportunity to discuss how one determines whether an excuse is a justification or an alibi.

The second relationship is that of fellow professional to acting professional. This differs from teacher—student professional primarily in that the two professionals are now on an equal footing in both status and knowledge. Although there is no role responsibility for instruction, there is a tradition of cooperation and sharing, particularly in the area of the profession's technical expertise. A fellow professional will often be a co-worker, but may be just a member of the profession who happens to observe activity where there are serious ethical considerations.

A fellow professional has advantages in fulfilling the role of someone who hears excuses and can evaluate whether they are valid or not. He has the experience and background to understand the context, the technical expertise required, and the various pressures placed on the actor. Therefore, he can best understand the nature of the duty, the breach, and the validity of the excuse. His comments would be most helpful in deciding whether the excuse is a justification or an alibi.

Is the observing professional free to ignore unethical activity by the actor? All professionals suffer from the public perception that professionals are unethical. One might take the position that being ethical in his own practice completely fulfills the professional's responsibility. Without some feedback and reaction from his fellows, however, can he be confident that he is always acting ethically? Our obligation goes beyond being ethical in our own actions. Ethical responsibility arises in those situations where we could have acted and thereby saved someone from injury. When we observe a professional abusing a client, should we not act the same way we ought to when we see an adult abusing a child? The question of when one has a duty to intervene is complicated because relationships are often private and personal. The parties may define their relationship differently from the way others would in what appears on the surface to be a similar relationship. One must be sure that the ethical abuse goes beyond acceptable choices by individuals with different sets of values or beyond the defensible exercise of professional judgment. The fact that it is difficult to know when and how to intervene does not excuse the fellow professional from interceding in egregious situations. Nor does it excuse the fellow professional from a teaching and counseling responsibility toward those who are acting unethically.

An additional complication occurs if the observing professional is a competitor. Raising ethical questions about the activity of the actor may represent mixed motives. The observer is opening himself up to the charge of trying to harass a competitor. That is an excuse for not intervening, but like most excuses not always justified.

To expect fellow professionals to perform this role requires weakening the grip of the informal moral rules that "One should mind one's own business" and "One should not hurt another's feelings." This is not to suggest these are unimportant principles, but, as in most ethical dilemmas in the real world, they must be balanced with the duty that the fellow professional owes. What is needed here is a more complex understanding of what constitutes one's own business. We must develop a tradition that helping fellow professionals solve their ethical problems is not invasive or improper.

Perhaps the most important relationship for analyzing excuses is that between professional actor and client. Shortly after World War II, Albert Camus, active in the resistance to the German occupation and an acute observer of the problems in Europe leading up to and during World War II, wrote an essay titled *Neither Victims nor Executioners*.[3] There he argued that one has a duty to occupy that narrow moral ground where one does not abuse or exploit others, but at the same time refuses to be exploited. Ethics tends to focus on the actor. Camus, as someone who had been oppressed, wanted to also consider the victim's responsibility. Refusing to be a victim means in part that one demands excuses and explanations for actions that harm him and scrutinizes those carefully to see whether they are persuasive.

The final relationship is that between the professional and those observers who are neither mentor, coprofessional, nor client. This would often be the person most likely to occupy an objective, disinterested position and whose opinion should be closest to that of the society as a whole, that is, the general public. To the extent the profession suffers from a reputation for being unethical, it is the observations and opinions of this group that are most influential. They will often learn of excuses given for unethical activity, and if they are suspicious, the excuse will not be persuasive, at least in raising public esteem of the actor and of her profession.

We are not isolated and totally autonomous individuals, but always part of relationships and groups. This social involvement requires being interested in what other people who are important to us do. We must be concerned about the ethical implications of their action. That is not easy to do. Recall the exchange with George Hole presented in Chapter 3 under the excuse "an act of kindness."[4] Compassion for colleagues who are performing in substandard fashion can lead us to condone and cover actions that harm clients and third persons. However, to expect a professional to monitor the actions of colleagues and to remonstrate with them when they appear unethical is asking a great deal. It seems to violate the valuable virtue of group loyalty, it requires us to act in ways that often appear unkind to colleagues who are having personal, psychological, or physical problems, and it invites reciprocal monitoring of our own actions, which might embarrass us and which we prefer to keep private.

Any adequate reaction to unpersuasive excuses given by unethical professionals requires surrendering that extreme version of autonomy and individualism that has plagued much of our current political and social analysis. We are social animals. Our relationships with people, particularly those with whom we work closely, are critical to our well-being. Can we not learn to think of the group as sufficiently important so we should share our concerns and work out our problems together, including solving ethical dilemmas that affect the group, not just the individual? We have grown accustomed to group therapy where personal difficulties are examined in the case of psychological problems, but do not extend that easily to ethical problems. Many of us have been raised with an attitude that it is a weakness to confess to problems or share them with other people. A healthier attitude would turn discussions of individual behavior, that creates a problem for the group away from pure criticism into a more constructive way of trying to solve ethical difficulties. These are often problems other members of the group are privately struggling with as well, so an open and frank discussion will alleviate much internal distress as well as lead toward better solutions.

When should the common excuses used by professionals for actions of disputed morality be thought of as mere alibis rather than genuine justifications? If others appear indifferent, that leaves the decision to the professional herself. In the present period of conflicting and diverse values, there are seldom clear theoretical answers for precise contexts of choice. Even when an accepted general principle seems applicable, the problems of applying it leave much ambiguity. If the professional thinks the excuse is appropriate, whether from rationalization, ignorance, or on valid grounds, she feels free to act against the standard.[5] The reality testing of that judgment might be the reaction of fellow professionals. However, many, if not most, professionals are reluctant to criticize fellow professionals' actions partly out of professional courtesy and partly as a protective device. They believe refraining from criticizing other professionals will encourage those others to abstain from criticizing them. Another reality test—at least at the borderlines where professional codes of ethics are at work—is whether some professional or legal sanction will be sought. For amoral professionals concerned only with consequences, that likelihood is not great enough to effectively inhibit self-interested justifications even for gross violations of ethical standards.[6]

If ethical professionals and professional groups want to limit the use of questionable excuses to justify unethical action, they must make known their disagreement with an unpersuasive excuse given by an actor in a particular context. They, however, have their own set of excuses used to avoid having to react in ways that would serve as an important reality check on the use of excuses by unethical practitioners. Among those are the claim of group loyalty, kindness toward fellow professionals, and the reciprocity of tolerance. A professional who uses one of these excuses to justify acquiescence with unethical activity of fellow professionals is himself acting unethically.

In order to develop our ethical expectations in detail and to work out the operation of acceptable excuses, we need more dialogue. There is, of course, substantial discussion now about ethics and some mention of excuses, but the quality and thoroughness of that discussion have to change. The dialogue that will move us forward should be more than academic, partly because we do not know enough about the contemporary contexts of duty, responsibility, excuses, guilt, and blame to give theoretical discussions the factual grounding they need. The dialogue must be between ordinary people facing the difficult problems they have to struggle with in their lives. When that dialogue does occur, we pay too little attention and do not take it seriously enough.

This dialogue about responsibility and excuses begins for all of us in childhood and occurs constantly whenever we are accused of some form of wrongdoing. When accused, it seems natural to offer an excuse. Sometimes, it will be outright false or unpersuasive. If such an excuse succeeds in avoiding punishment, or more accurately, the ascription of responsibility that must precede punishment, a questionable pattern is being set up, which is reinforced every time the process works. Very few parents or teachers, particularly in the high-pressure world of today, take the time to listen to a child's excuse and discuss whether it is valid or not. The child is likely to get one of two responses from busy and preoccupied parents. The first is to regularly disbelieve all excuses as lies or alibis. In such an exchange, the child gradually learns that the excuse is pro forma and never really works; that is, the child is always wrong. The other common response is that the parent accepts the excuse because it avoids the time-consuming and difficult job of assessing its validity. To evaluate an excuse seriously calls for a process with some of the qualities of a trial at law. There must be an assessment of the factual validity of the excuse and some judgment about its normative value. If true, is it a legitimate justification? Such a procedure, as any lawyer knows, is not an easy one.

The tendency to choose the easy way out, that is, to avoid difficult questions, is well established even in legal procedures. Both the formation of a legal rule and the process of applying it often have as their real rationale the relative ease and efficiency of applying the rule and resolving the dispute. If difficult questions could be avoided by accepting one version of a rule over the other, the administratively easy rule would be the one most likely chosen.[7] While it is an understandable human reaction to avoid difficulties, improvement in ethical behavior requires facing up to tough questions, not avoiding them.

This process of giving short shrift to excuses continues in adulthood. The predilection of many people today is to just accept an excuse without quibbling, first, because it avoids the implications of disbelieving valued acquaintances, second, because it is unnecessary to spend time in making difficult decisions about factual accuracy and normative validity, and finally because one does not have to make tough decisions about how to react if one finds the excuse invalid. Does one express disapproval and dislike of the actor who may be an important figure in one's life? Does one shun the actor? Does one complain to others or publicize the problem?

What is needed is more regular and candid discussion about excuses on a daily basis. It is here that the skills, attitudes, and procedures of the lawyer may be most dangerous. Over the centuries Anglo-American lawyers have learned to treat human disputes as conflicts where one party must prevail and we therefore need to decide which one was right. Lawyers have only tentatively begun to expand their expertise to include alternative forms of dispute resolution, such as mediation and arbitration. It is in these processes of compromise rather than litigational or confrontational attitudes that the sort of discussion could occur that would clarify the role of excuses. This ongoing discussion is necessary if we are to improve the issue of responsibility in a changing and complex world.

The obligation of observers (and victims) to react to unethical activity by professionals is not a call for watchdog or monitoring activity so much as a request to bring issues out in the open and discuss them in a cooperative and understanding way. We are all sometimes actors, sometimes victims, and sometime observers. If any of these roles would benefit from such discussions, then all of us should willingly participate.

There are important differences between the dialogue that ought to go on between fellow professionals and that between professional and victim. An excuse can be given to either. The value of discussion with a fellow professional is she can put herself in the actor's shoes, understanding the technical and ethical complexities of the problem of choice faced by the actor. The fellow professional's reaction is a good reality check for the actor. If his excuse does not persuade his fellow professional that the action was proper, he should reexamine his own evaluations and change his conduct accordingly.

As between a professional who has acted wrongfully and an injured victim, the giving and evaluating of excuses is a kind of negotiation as to whether the act should be condoned or pardoned. The victim's reaction to the excuse is an essential part of this process of explanation, atonement, and forgiveness. One problem with a professional's complete acceptance of the victim's evaluation as to whether his excuse is an alibi or a justification is that the victim, who is often not a professional and very rarely a professional with the special expertise of the actor, will seldom be able to sympathetically understand all the complexities of choice faced by the actor. Nor is the victim disinterested in his evaluation. The victim has been injured in some way and blames the professional. His evaluation of excuses given by the professional, and there will almost always be excuses given for conduct the client is unhappy with, may well be overcritical.

The discussion following the giving of an excuse, particularly between the actor and alleged victim, fulfills a number of functions. This, of course, presupposes that the discussion is genuine and not perfunctory.

The first is to clarify the issues of responsibility and behind that, the question of obligation. The giving of an excuse and having it accepted or rejected is a part of deciding whether the excuse is a justification or an alibi and thus whether the actor has a responsibility. It also defines the zones of operation of an ethical principle. Was the conduct clearly covered by the principle? Was it in the gray area surrounding the principle, that is, a penumbral problem? Or was it definitely outside the purpose of the principle? It is only by considering these questions in a number of different cases that one really begins to understand the scope of particular ethical principles.

The second function is to learn more about the practical details of responsibility. We need a better understanding of both the theoretical and practical role of excuses and neither of these is a purely academic matter. J. L. Austin in his classic "A Plea for Excuses" looked at ordinary language as the best clue to the functioning of excuses and obviously behind that lies ordinary experience.

The third, an extremely important function, is the relief of guilt, which is more a psychological than an analytical function. The process of atonement and forgiveness must take place or else guilt increases and piles up until it is psychologically unbearable. We all know the experience of doing something we probably should not have and feeling that someone we care about will blame us for that action. The giving of an excuse and having it accepted by that significant other person is an enormous relief. It eases that portion of guilt attributable to the particular indiscretion that, in the absence of forgiveness, would otherwise remain and fester. When a professional has done something that injures a client and for which he himself takes blame, at least internally, the client saying: "I understand," "It's all right," or "I forgive you" provides the same sort of relief. The relief cannot, however, be of the quality of "I got away with it" or "I evaded responsibility," but rather an acceptance of responsibility and guilt, then an atonement or forgiveness that restores the equilibrium, and finally a serious attempt not to engage in that particular unethical activity again.

In many cultures, this is the appropriate time for an apology, accepting responsibility and showing remorse. In North America, we are inclined more to the approach of avoiding responsibility through excuse, rather than accepting it and apologizing. The existence of the possibility, if not the probability, of a legal action by the victim increases the disinclination to apologize, because it might appear to be an admission not only of ethical responsibility, but of legal guilt as well. This is one important reason why the provision of insurance protection discussed in the preceding chapter ought to be unlinked from the question of legal responsibility. Only then can the process of apology and forgiveness freely occur.

There are difficulties with expecting professionals to not only give excuses, but be willing to discuss them seriously with clients. The first is a natural human reluctance, at least in our culture, to openly admit possible error or wrongdoing. That is particularly difficult for successful professionals who have a high opinion of themselves and often with reason. The second problem is the time cost. The time of professionals is valuable and more so if we are talking about successful professionals. The time spent in giving excuses and carefully discussing them with clients does not seem to be productive time financially or not as productive as performing professional services for other clients. That claim of not being able to afford the time has to be met head-on. There is an ethical and professional responsibility to adequately justify one's services to a client. Second, there is a distinction between short-term and long-term gain. A satisfied client is not only less likely to bring a malpractice action, but more likely to bring new business to the professional either personally or through references.

If discussion is brought to a halt because the excuse offered by the professional is rejected by a client-victim, what does one do at that point? One possibility is to call in an objective observer, not necessarily to decide the case, but rather to serve as impartial observer and mediator. This person may well be a professional, but need not be. The client may feel professionals stick together and therefore distrust the objectivity of someone in the same position as the professional actor. It might be possible to develop a group of experts to perform this role who are trained in mediation and understand excuses and how they should be dealt with.

Another important need is to develop some method of allowing the discussion and resolution of interesting or unusual contexts to be shared with others, so this process of working out problems in a particular context need not be repeated again and again. That is a lesson to be learned from the legal system. The common law process of deciding each case and then recording it so that judges and parties need not rework the same ground has produced much insight into and evolution of sound rules and sound defenses in individual disputes.

There is now a record of proceedings by ethics committees of professional associations, but that is limited to claimed violations of the formal code and does not reflect the natural process of participants working out their common view of the duties and the excuses in particular contexts. Instead, they are the legal or quasi-legal resolution by formal committees of the profession. It is hard to develop and design ways of keeping a record of the informal processes of dispute resolution and a method of disseminating those results for the information of others who may face the same problem. I do not wish to attempt that now, but merely to show the desirability of such a process as a way of improving our understanding of excuses and their critical role in developing our understanding of responsibility in the contemporary world. If we were to develop a group of expert mediators to deal with the dialogue around excuses, one of the by-products of their efforts could be to record and share the experiences of discussing excuses with professionals and victims in specific problem contexts.

The ongoing discussion of these matters should prevent us when we are actors from using alibis or unpersuasive excuses, as well as when we are victims from accepting alibis and thereby not blaming the unethical actor. It is also important not to absolve observers who stand idly by while the level of unethical activity in our professions and our lives increases.

Like all dialogues, there have to be two active participants. Either the professional or the victim can initiate the dialogue. The professional should be sure that the excuse is both understood and accepted. The victim should not accept alibis, but insist on real explanations.

It may seem that a social process that goes on daily between all members of the society and that tends to tolerate excuses that undercut responsibility for one's unethical actions cannot be easily reversed or reformed. It is not, however, a process that is fixed, but is constantly being used and adapted to the needs of particular contexts, peoples, and times. That is why the focus on professionals is significant. First, there is the explicit commitment to being ethical, which should certainly encompass not using invalid excuses to avoid responsibility for unethical activity. Second, professionals occupy positions of influence and power in the society. If the legal profession, the medical profession, the teaching profession, and the journalistic profession, among others, would commit themselves to genuine discussions of these issues whenever they are accused of acting unethically, that would start a process of reversing the use of unjustified excuses or alibis.[8] Then, of course, most professionals are also parents and neighbors who, if they brought this style of discussion into all their relationships, not just their professional ones, would have an important and fairly immediate impact on the giving, assessing, and accepting or rejecting excuses.

NOTES

1. See Banks McDowell, "The Ethical Obligations of Professional Teachers (of Ethics)," PROFESSIONAL ETHICS: A MULTIDISCIPLINARY JOURNAL, Vol. 1, Nos. 3 & 4 (1992): 53.

2. My preference as a teacher was to give students wide latitude in structuring their own learning and defining their own tasks. This made it hard for me to set fixed guidelines and to require performance, the failure of which, would require excuses. See Banks McDowell, "The Dilemma of a (Law) Teacher, 52 BOSTON

UNIVERSITY LAW REVIEW 247 (1972). This has made it difficult for me to fulfill this duty I now say belongs to the role of the teacher.

3. Albert Camus, NEITHER VICTIMS NOR EXECUTIONERS, 1946, Reprint (Chicago: N.A. 1972).

4. Pp. 75–77.

5. To the extent that the actor represses that he is performing an unethical act, it raises serious questions of self-awareness. See John J. McDermott, "Pragmatic Sensibility: The Morality of Experience," in Joseph P. DeMarco and Richard M. Fox, NEW DIRECTIONS IN ETHICS: THE CHALLENGE OF APPLIED ETHICS (New York and London: Routledge & Kegan Paul, 1986), p. 122: "The moral question which dogs us in our human activity is forever sullied if we live a life of self-deception. To the contrary, the task is to face up to the deepest paradox in our lives, namely, that our decisons are of paramount importance, though they have no ultimate future to sanction them."

6. Here, I am again using Holmes's "bad man" analysis. See Chapter 4, Note 10.

7. An interesting example of the use of administrative convenience by the legal system occurs in *Frontiero v. Richardson*, 411 U.S. 677, 93 S.Ct. 1764, 36 L.Ed.2d 583 (1973). Congress had enacted statutes that provided that a serviceman could claim housing and health benefits for his wife whether she was dependent on him or not. A servicewoman could claim such benefits for her spouse only if he were in fact dependent. When these statutes were challenged, the government defended them by claiming that since the vast majority of service personnel were male and that most of them were the breadwinners in the family, it was administratively convenient to apply a presumption of dependence, but in the case of service-women, Congress intended a factual determination. The Supreme Court of the United States, while noting that speed and efficiency were important values, said they could not override an interest entitled to strict scrutiny. The statutes were held to violate due process.

8. A contemporary example of this process is the case of Joe Klein, a journalist who wrote the best-selling *Primary Colors* under the pseudonym "Anonymous." He publicly and frequently denied, including to his co-workers, that he was "Anonymous." When he was discovered to be the actual author, he apologized profusely, but was considered by most journalists to have acted unethically.

11

Conclusion

Just as a lawyer who does not know the legal defenses is not a competent lawyer, so an ethicist who does not understand the ethical excuses can hardly be said to fully understand his area of expertise. An ethical theory that does not account for excuses is incomplete. Excuses are so much a part of our daily discourse and relationships with each other that we probably take them as much for granted as the air we breathe. Unfortunately, we have thought, talked, or written too little about excuses. One reason why we have not taken up the invitation of J. L. Austin to investigate excuses is because of its difficulties.

The first is a descriptive one. Just what excuses are actually being used and from among those, which ones are persuasive or valid? Since ethics is largely a system of voluntary compliance and those actors who do not comply try to hide their non-compliance not only from others but from themselves, they may not be personally aware they are acting unethically or that they are using excuses for themselves. Getting excuses out in the open and getting them labeled is a preliminary first step to discovering how often and in what ways they are used. That requires more open discussion about the validity of excuses among the actors who are giving excuses, victims who have been harmed by the unethical action, those observers who are witnesses, and by ethical theorists.

The second difficulty is linguistic. Excuses carry a negative connotation. We may avoid talking about excuses because we think any time an excuse is used, we are avoiding responsibility in a questionable way. Excuses, however, have value in pointing out difficult social and personal problems and also have great utility in dealing with the pervasive problems of application: problems of penumbral coverage, flexibility, and unavoidable human error.

Focusing on excuses and trying to understand them opens up a number of deeper problems with the operation of ethics, particularly in practical areas, such as professional practice.

The first is that theory is too often created without a sufficiently clear or current picture of the real world in which it must operate. We may not like the world we live in or at least many features of it, but we have little choice except to live inside that world. We can talk grandly about changing the structure of professions or the way professionals work, and I have done some of that in this book, but institutions and practices are often adapted to a kind of functioning fit with the world we live in and cannot be easily changed in fundamental ways.

A second problem is that the world is in great flux and so it is difficult both to understand the contemporary world and to make predictions as to how it is developing. Some twenty-five years ago, when I was chairman of the faculty senate at Boston University and caught between a militant faculty and an autocratic university president, I was suffering through one of the worst periods of my life. On different occasions, sympathetic colleagues from around the university in an attempt to cheer me up reminded me of an ancient Chinese curse, "May you live in a time of great change." I was never quite sure why that was supposed to make me feel better. All of us who have lived in the second half of the twentieth century are subject to that curse. As a consequence, one must be cautious about trying to draw long-term generalizations.

Given the uncertainty about the contemporary reality and the rate of change in it, we must be wary about simple models on which to build any theory to understand contemporary problems. The two-person model of conventional ethics is of limited value because we are entangled in a web of relationships. What works well for one relationship often has a devastating effect on others. One example is the dedicated doctor who is always there for his patients and so his family suffers because of that commitment.

One must also reject a perfectionist's view of ethics. It is not in human nature to be perfect. As the Christian ethic tells us, we are all sinners. As our common sense tells us, we are all fallible and make mistakes. If we are intelligent, we learn from mistakes and do not continue to repeat them, but mistakes we will always make. Any practical and workable professional ethics must come to terms with that fallibility. Excuses are one important way of giving any ethical system sufficient flexibility so that everybody, including the most conscientious and capable, is not damned to eternal guilt.

In "A Plea for Excuses,"[1] an address delivered in 1956, J. L. Austin thought that he had only opened up the subject of "excuses." A much more detailed study would enlighten the entire area of responsibility and what it means to act or not to act.[2] In the professional arena, the existence of excuses and the amount of unethical and self-serving activity by practitioners suggest that fundamental problems that are masked by excuses still need to be addressed. The existence and wide use of excuses to evade personal responsibility coupled with other factors, such as defining ethics as limited to establishing borderlines of acceptable conduct and training professionals to be specialists who possess technical expertise rather than certain ethical traits, have marginalized professional ethics. The existence of a ready and acceptable set of excuses, however, is at the core of this marginalization. Until we deal more forthrightly with these issues, the current emphasis on professional ethics will remain largely a public-relations gambit rather than a real improvement in professional integrity.

Ultimately, the problem facing practical ethics is to develop ways of achieving balances between competing, if not conflicting, obligations as well as coming to terms with constraints that are hard to ignore. There are conflicting duties owed to obligees, not only clients, but also friends, families, and associates. There are the needs to perform competently as technical professionals in a world of great pressures and changes. There is the ambition to achieve a high level of excellence at a time when we are under enormous personal stress. There are desires to be decent in a world that is so cynical it no longer seems to value the old ethical virtues. Excuses are the focal point where these conflicts all come to the surface and we ignore their clues only at great personal and social risk.

NOTES

1. J. L. Austin, "A Please for Excuses," PHILOSOPHICAL PAPERS, 3d ed. (New York: Oxford University Press, 1979).

2. According to G. J. Warnock, J. L. AUSTIN (London and New York: Routledge, 1992), pp. 65–66, Austin was compressing into the some thirty pages of this article a whole series of classes or seminars. The discussion had of necessity to be compact focusing on important questions and leaving much of the complexity, some of the answers, and almost all of the reasons for the answers out of the presentation. Unfortunately, neither Austin nor anyone since that time has provided this development in an accessible form.

Bibliography

Abbott, Andrew. THE SYSTEM OF PROFESSIONS: AN ESSAY ON THE DIVISION OF EXPERT LABOR. Chicago: The University of Chicago Press, 1988.

American Law Institute. MODEL PENAL CODE, § 204.

———. RESTATEMENT OF THE LAW OF TORTS, SECOND, §§ 8, 402A, 1965.

Austin, J. L., "A Plea for Excuses," PHILOSOPHICAL PAPERS, 3d ed., New York: Oxford University Press, 1979, p. 181.

———. "Three Ways of Spilling Ink." PHILOSOPHICAL PAPERS, 3d ed., New York: Oxford University Press, 1979.

Bates v. State Bar of Arizona, 433 U.S. 350 (1977).

Becker, Ernest. THE DENIAL OF DEATH. New York: Free Press, 1973.

Berger, Joseph. "The Long Days and Short Life of a Medical Student: Relatives Say Fatigue May Have Had a Role in the Car Crash that Killed Frank Ingulli." NEW YORK TIMES, Sunday, May 30, 1993, Sec. 1, p. 39, col. 2.

Berlin, Isaiah. FOUR ESSAYS ON LIBERTY. London: Oxford University Press, 1969.

Brink, Andre. "The Writer as Witch," in Miller Christ, ed., THE DISSIDENT WORD; THE OXFORD AMNESTY LECTURES 1995. New York: Basic Books, 1996.

Camus, Albert. NEITHER VICTIMS NOR EXECUTIONERS, 1946, Reprint. Chicago: N.A. 1972.

Clark, Kathleen. "Do We Have Enough Ethics in Government Yet?" UNIVERSITY OF ILLINOIS LAW REVIEW (February 1996): 58–63.

Corbin, Arthur L. CORBIN ON CONTRACTS. St. Paul, Minn.: West Publishing Co., 1960.

———. "Legal Analysis and Terminology," 29 YALE LAW JOURNAL (1919): 163–173.

Dawson, John P., William Burnett Harvey, and Stanley D. Henderson. CASES AND COMMENT ON CONTRACTS, 5th ed., Brooklyn: The Foundation Press, 1987.

DeMarco, Joseph P. and Richard M. Fox. NEW DIRECTIONS IN ETHICS: THE CHALLENGE OF APPLIED ETHICS. New York and London: Routledge & Kegan Paul, 1986.

Dworkin, Ronald. TAKING RIGHTS SERIOUSLY. Cambridge, Mass.: Harvard University Press, 1978.

Ellul, Jacques. THE TECHNOLOGICAL SOCIETY. New York: Vintage Books, 1964.

Feinberg, Joel. DOING AND DESERVING: ESSAYS IN THE THEORY OF RESPONSIBILITY. Princeton: Princeton University Press, 1970.

Firestone v. Crown Center Redevelopment Corporation, 693 S.W.2d (Mo. en banc,1985).

Fish, Stanley. THERE'S NO SUCH THING AS FREE SPEECH . . . AND IT'S A GOOD THING TOO. New York: Oxford University Press, 1994.

Fletcher, George P. RETHINKING CRIMINAL LAW. Boston: Little, Brown, 1978.

Fortas, Abe. CONCERNING DISSENT AND CIVIL DISOBEDIENCE. New York: New American Library, 1968.

Fowler, Elizabeth M., "Reducing the Stress on Lawyers." NEW YORK TIMES, Jan. 23, 1990, p. C17.

Frontiero v. Richardson, 411 U.S. 677 (1973).

Fuller, Lon L. THE MORALITY OF LAW. New Haven: Yale University Press, 1964.

———. THE PROBLEMS OF JURISPRUDENCE, temporary edition. Brooklyn: The Foundation Press, 1949.

———. "Positivism and Fidelity to Law—A Reply to Professor Hart." 71 HARVARD LAW REVIEW 630 (1958).

Fuller, Lon L. and Melvin Eisenberg. BASIC CONTRACT LAW. St. Paul, Minn.: West Publishing Co., 1972.

Fuller, Lon L. and William Perdue. "The Reliance Interest in Contract Damages," 46 YALE LAW JOURNAL 52 (1936).

Gadd, Jane. "MD Reporting of Threats Wins Backing," THE GLOBE AND MAIL, Toronto, Tuesday, July 11, 1996, p. A3.

Gorovitz, Samuel. DOCTORS' DILEMMAS: MORAL CONFLICT AND MEDICAL CARE. New York: Macmillan, 1982.

Guggenberger, Bernd. DAS MENSCHENRECHT AUF IRRTUM. Munich and Vienna: Carl Hanswer Verlag, 1987.

Hamilton, Robert W., Alan Scott Rau, and Russell J. Weintraub. CASES AND MATERIALS ON CONTRACTS, 2d ed. St. Paul, Minn.: West Publishing Co., 1992.

Hampshire, Stuart. "Public and Private Morality," in PUBLIC AND PRIVATE MORALITY, Stuart Hampshire, ed., Cambridge: Cambridge University Press, 1978.

Hart, H.L.A. THE CONCEPT OF LAW. Oxford: Clarendon Press, 1961.

———. "Positivism and the Separation of Law and Morals," 71 HARVARD LAW REVIEW 593 (1958).

Hohfeld, Wesley N. FUNDAMENTAL LEGAL CONCEPTIONS. New Haven: Yale University Press, 1919.

Holmes, Oliver Wendell, Jr. "The Path of the Law," 10 HARVARD LAW REVIEW 457 (1897).

Jacobs, Jane. THE DEATH AND LIFE OF GREAT AMERICAN CITIES. New York: Vintage Books, 1961.

———. SYSTEMS OF SURVIVAL: A DIALOGUE ON THE MORAL FOUNDA-TIONS OF COMMERCE AND POLITICS. New York: Vintage Books, 1992.

Keeton, Robert and Alan Widiss. INSURANCE LAW, 2d ed. St. Paul, Minn.: West Publishing Co., 1988.

"Killer of Abortion Doctor Is Sentenced to Die," NEW YORK TIMES, Wednesday, December 7, 1994, p. A16.

Landress v. Phoenix Ins. Co., 291 U.S. 499 (1933).

Lasch, Christopher. THE CULTURE OF NARCISSISM: AMERICAN LIFE IN AN AGE OF DIMINISHING EXPECTATIONS. New York: Warner Books, 1979.

Luban, David and Michael Millemann. "Good Judgment: Ethics Teaching in Dark Times." 9 GEORGETOWN JOURNAL OF LEGAL ETHICS 31 (1995).

Marron, Kevin. "Lawyers Wary as Multinationals Eye Their Turf." THE GLOBE AND MAIL, Toronto, August 12, 1997, p. B27.

McDermott, John J. "Pragmatic Sensibility: The Morality of Experience," in De-marco and Fox, NEW DIRECTIONS IN ETHICS: THE CHALLENGE OF APPLIED ETHICS, New York and London: Routledge & Kegan Paul, 1986.

McDowell, Banks. "Causation in Contracts and Insurance." 20 CONNECTICUT LAW REVIEW 569 (1988).

———. DEREGULATION AND COMPETITION IN THE INSURANCE INDUS-TRY. Westport, Conn.: Quorum Books, 1989.

———. "The Dilemma of a (Law) Teacher." 52 BOSTON UNIVERSITY LAW RE-VIEW 247 (1972).

———. ETHICAL CONDUCT AND THE PROFESSIONAL'S DILEMMA: CHOOSING BETWEEN SERVICE AND SUCCESS. Westport, Conn.: Quorum Books, 1991.

———. "The Ethical Obligations of Professional Teachers (of Ethics)." PROFES-SIONAL ETHICS: A MULTIDISCIPLINARY JOURNAL, Vol. 1, Nos. 3 & 4 (1992).

———. "Foreseeability in Contract and Tort: The Problems of Responsibility and Remoteness." 36 CASE WESTERN RESERVE LAW REVIEW 286 (1985).

———. "Lawyers as Manipulators: Is This a Model for Legal Education?" 31 WASHBURN LAW REVIEW 506 (1992).

———. "The Misrepresentation Defense in Insurance: A Problem for Contract Theory." 16 CONNECTICUT LAW REVIEW 513 (1984).

Mills v. Wyman, 3 Pick. 207 (Mass., 1826).

Morgan Thomas D. and Rotunda, Ronald D., eds. MODEL CODE OF PROFES-SIONAL RESPONSIBILITY, MODEL RULES OF PROFESSIONAL CON-DUCT AND OTHER SELECTED STANDARDS, Mineola, N.Y., Foundation Press, 1996.

Nagel, Thomas. "Ruthlessness in Public Life," in PUBLIC AND PUBLIC MORAL-ITY, Stuart Hampshire, ed. Cambridge: Cambridge University Press, 1978.

Pear, Robert. "Clinton Advisers Outline a Big Shift for Malpractice." NEW YORK TIMES, Friday, May 21, 1983, P. A1, col. 6.

Perez-Pena, Richard. "New York to Drop Clifford Charges." NEW YORK TIMES, Tuesday, November 2, 1993, p. B7.

Perkins, Rollin M. CRIMINAL LAW. Brooklyn: The Foundation Press, 1957.

Prosser, William L. HANDBOOK OF THE LAW OF TORTS, 4th ed. St. Paul, Minn.: West Publishing Co., 1971.

Rawls, John. A THEORY OF JUSTICE. Cambridge, Mass.: Harvard University Press, 1972.

Rhode, Deborah. "Moral Character as a Professional Credential." 94 YALE LAW JOURNAL 491 (1985).

Rovere, Richard H. HOWE AND HUMMEL: THEIR TRUE AND SCANDALOUS HISTORY. New York: Farrar, Straus, 1947.

Saul, John Ralston. THE UNCONSCIOUS CIVILIZATION. Concord, Ont.: House of Anansi Press, 1995.

Scanlon, T. M. "Rights, Goals and Fairness," in PUBLIC AND PRIVATE MORAL-ITY, Stuart Hampshire, ed. Cambridge: Cambridge University Press, 1978.

Seelye, Katherine Q. "Packwood Resigns Senate Seat After Panel Details Evidence," NEW YORK TIMES, Friday, September 8, 1995, p. A1, col. 6.

Shapero v. Kentucky Bar Assn., 486 U.S. 466 (1988).

Sherwood v. Walker, 66 Mich. 568, 33 N.W. 919 (1887).

Stryker, Lloyd Paul. FOR THE DEFENSE: THOMAS ERSKINE, THE MOST EN-LIGHTENED LIBERAL OF HIS TIMES, 1750–1823, Garden City, N.Y.: Doubleday, 1947.

Thomas, Ross. CHINAMAN'S CHANCE. New York: Warner Books, 1978.

———. OUT ON THE RIM. New York: Warner Books, 1987.

———. VOODOO, LTD. New York: Warner Books, 1992.

Warnock, G. L., J. L. AUSTIN. London and New York: Routledge, 1991.

Wolff, Robert Paul. THE IDEAL OF THE UNIVERSITY. Boston: Beacon Press, 1969.

Zinn, Howard. DISOBEDIENCE AND DEMOCRACY: NINE FALLACIES ON LAW AND ORDER. New York: Random House, 1968.

Index

About the Author

BANKS McDOWELL is Professor Emeritus, Washburn University School of Law. Earlier he was Austin B. Fletcher Professor of Law at Boston University, and held other positions on the faculties of Syracuse University and the University of Tulsa. Among his various publications are three books with Quorum: *Deregulation and Competition in the Insurance Industry* (1989), *Ethical Conduct and the Professional's Dilemma* (1991), and *The Crisis in Insurance Regulation* (1994).